ANDREW JACKSON

OUR
FEDERAL UNION
IT
MUST BE PRESERVED.

FIRST EDITION
© 1963 by American Heritage Publishing Co., Inc., 551 Fifth Ave., N.Y. 17, N.Y. All rights reserved under
Berne and Pan-American Copyright Conventions. Library of Congress Catalog Card Number: 63 15123.

SOLDIER AND STATESMAN

FRANKLIN D. ROOSEVELT LIBRARY

BY THE EDITORS OF
AMERICAN HERITAGE
The Magazine of History

AUTHOR
RALPH K. ANDRIST

CONSULTANT
ARTHUR M. SCHLESINGER, JR.
Author of THE AGE OF JACKSON

PUBLISHED BY
AMERICAN HERITAGE
PUBLISHING CO., INC.
New York

BOOK TRADE AND INSTITUTIONAL DISTRIBUTION BY
HARPER & ROW

Jackson the warrior, painted by Ralph E. W. Earl in 1833.

Foreword

In the decade of the 1820's Americans were flexing their muscles and looking for new fields to conquer. Within fifty years they had won a revolution, established a new form of government, and survived a second conflict, the War of 1812, with the armies of Great Britain. New settlements sprang up like weeds beyond the Appalachian Mountains, and new factories appeared in the older eastern states. The people of this explosive era took a hard look at their political leaders and decided it was time for a changing of the guard.

Until 1828 the American Presidency was the preserve of men from either Virginia or Massachusetts, the bedrock states of the Republic. These were men of intellect and cool reason; now the people wanted a man of action. They elected Andrew Jackson of Tennessee, war hero and spokesman for the frontier, the first President from west of the Alleghenies, the first born in a log cabin.

Andrew Jackson had literally fought his way to the White House. As a youngster he battled the British during the Revolution, and all his life he never stopped fighting—against opponents in rough frontier politics, against the British in the War of 1812, against Indians at all times.

One of Jackson's chief political opponents, Henry Clay, could not believe "that the killing of 2,500 Englishmen at New Orleans qualifies a person for the various, difficult, and complicated duties" of the Presidency. But Daniel Webster, the great senator from Massachusetts, saw the Jacksonian revolution more clearly. "When he comes," Webster wrote, "he will bring a breeze with him. . . ." A breeze indeed; Jackson plunged into the Presidency with both fists swinging. He fought to expand the powers of his office, to break the monopoly of a national bank, to halt the threat of secession that endangered the Union.

This was the era when the political cartoon came of age, and, as the samples in this book indicate, the cartoonists did not spare Old Hickory. For him or against him, everyone marveled at the old warrior's fighting spirit. When Andrew Jackson left the White House in 1837, he was seventy years old and broken in health, yet in the eight years left to him, he continued his fight for a stronger America. After Jackson's death, a friend tried to sum up his career. "His awful will," he wrote, "stood alone, & was made the will of all he commanded."

—The Editors

Six new AMERICAN HERITAGE JUNIOR LIBRARY *books are published each year. Titles currently available are:*

ANDREW JACKSON, SOLDIER AND STATESMAN

ADVENTURES IN THE WILDERNESS

LEXINGTON, CONCORD AND BUNKER HILL

CLIPPER SHIPS AND CAPTAINS

D-DAY, THE INVASION OF EUROPE

WESTWARD ON THE OREGON TRAIL

THE FRENCH AND INDIAN WARS

GREAT DAYS OF THE CIRCUS

STEAMBOATS ON THE MISSISSIPPI

COWBOYS AND CATTLE COUNTRY

TEXAS AND THE WAR WITH MEXICO

THE PILGRIMS AND PLYMOUTH COLONY

THE CALIFORNIA GOLD RUSH

PIRATES OF THE SPANISH MAIN

TRAPPERS AND MOUNTAIN MEN

MEN OF SCIENCE AND INVENTION

NAVAL BATTLES AND HEROES

THOMAS JEFFERSON AND HIS WORLD

DISCOVERERS OF THE NEW WORLD

RAILROADS IN THE DAYS OF STEAM

INDIANS OF THE PLAINS

THE STORY OF YANKEE WHALING

American Heritage also publishes HORIZON CARAVEL BOOKS, *a similar series on world history, culture, and the arts. Titles currently available are:*

JOAN OF ARC

EXPLORATION OF AFRICA

NELSON AND THE AGE OF FIGHTING SAIL

ALEXANDER THE GREAT

RUSSIA UNDER THE CZARS

HEROES OF POLAR EXPLORATION

KNIGHTS OF THE CRUSADES

COVER: *Thomas Sully's oil study of Andrew Jackson, painted about 1845, succeeds in capturing the heroic image of the most famous and popular American of his day.*

MELLON COLLECTION, NATIONAL GALLERY OF ART

ENDSHEETS: *Jackson, visible at left under the American flag, directs his troops at the Battle of New Orleans. This engraving was made from the painting on pages 78–79.*

MABEL BRADY GARVAN, YALE UNIVERSITY ART GALLERY

The Hermitage

Contents

ILLUSTRATED WITH PAINTINGS, PRINTS, PHOTO-
GRAPHS, DRAWINGS, AND MAPS OF THE PERIOD

Pioneers like those scratching out a meager living in this 1822 painting formed the backbone of Andrew Jackson's popular support. Many accepted his frontier birth as proof of their common destiny with him.

1 The Boy of the Waxhaws

There is an old story that even after Andrew Jackson had been dead for many years, people in the backwoods still went to the polls every election day and voted faithfully for Old Hickory for President.

It is a story that could almost be true. Merchants, bankers, land barons, and other men of property who wanted a secure and settled world considered Jackson at best a wild man from across the mountains and at worst an agent of the devil himself. But the common people—the pioneers in the raw new settlements west of the Appalachian Mountains, the workingmen in the raw new cities of the East—loved Andrew Jackson as one of themselves, and there were enough of them to elect him President twice.

And when they had elected him, he turned out to be, in the judgment of history, one of the five or six truly great American Presidents—although respectable people of his day did not

see him that way. He was not great because he was a learned man, for he was not; sometimes he was not even very wise. He was a famous Indian fighter, and he won a tremendous victory over the British in 1815, but being a great warrior does not necessarily mean a man will be a great President.

As for faults, Andrew Jackson had his share. He drank, swore, and gambled heavily, at least during his early years. He was quarrelsome and quick-tempered. His introduction of the spoils system (the awarding of government jobs to political party workers), while it brought new life and new people into government, was a device much abused until the Civil Service reforms a half-century later.

This is hardly the sort of record usually associated with a great President. Why, then, were his eight years in the White House so important to the young Republic? To answer that question requires an understanding

The task of hacking a farm out of the South's scrub pine forests demanded an iron will and a vision of better things to come. The raw homestead above, typical of its day, was drawn by a traveler in the early 19th century. A frontiersman's dream was the orderly South Carolina plantation at left, which was capable of producing immense crops by means of slave labor.

not only of Andrew Jackson himself but of the times in which he lived.

The parents of the future President were Andrew and Elizabeth Jackson who, with two very young sons, Hugh and Robert, came to America from northern Ireland in 1765. Elizabeth Jackson had four sisters who had already settled in a region on the border between North and South Carolina known as the Waxhaws; when the Jacksons made the difficult overland journey to the same district, they knew they would be among friends.

The Waxhaws, near the settled communities of that day, was an island of fertile soil amidst the region's scrub pine barrens. Elizabeth Jackson's sisters and their husbands had arrived several years earlier when there was still plenty of fine land to farm. All were doing well. But there was not much choice left by the time Andrew came. He had to take two hundred acres near the edge of the Waxhaws where the soil was thin and without much promise. Still he worked hard, and the yellowed records reveal that he had cleared some of his fields, built a log house, and raised at least one crop by the beginning of 1767.

But carving a farm out of this wilderness was brutally hard work. Eventually it killed him; early in 1767 he died at the age of twenty-nine, from severe strains suffered while trying to move a heavy log. His body was borne over a snowy track on a horse-drawn sled and buried in the churchyard at the hamlet of Waxhaw.

Less than two weeks after her husband's death, Elizabeth Jackson gave birth to her third son, and christened him Andrew after the father he never knew. North and South Carolina still dispute the honor of possessing the birthplace of Andrew Jackson. The boundary wiggles through the Waxhaws, and even when people who remembered those days were still alive, they could not agree which of the two sisters Elizabeth Jackson was staying with when her baby was born. If she was with one, the birthplace is in North Carolina, if with the other, in South Carolina.

Young Andrew worked hard as he grew up, but no harder than other boys of that time and place. Although his mother was a widow, there was something for every pair of hands to do in a frontier community, and Mrs. Jackson had an honorable place in the household of one of her sisters. Her children suffered no real hardship.

Young Andrew received as good an education as could be had in the Waxhaws, and in fact a considerably better one than most boys because his mother had her heart set on seeing him become a Presbyterian minister. Andrew, however, was no scholar. Although no one had to spend much time at school in such a settlement, he preferred running free with his friends to doing any studying whatsoever.

Throughout his life he remained a man of narrow education. He knew little of science, history, or literature, and his spelling was always a wonder to behold (even when he was President he might spell the same word three or four different ways in a letter). The one thing in which he excelled was reading.

In a frontier region like the Waxhaws, few people could read, and newspapers arrived very infrequently.

Horatio Gates (left) was credited with a major victory over the British at Saratoga in 1777; his inept leadership at Camden in 1780 nearly resulted in his court-martial.

Lt. Colonel Banastre "Butcher" Tarleton (right), boyishly handsome in this portrait, rode roughshod over southern patriots and became a hero in England for his exploits.

"I have cut 170 off'rs and men to pieces," wrote Colonel Tarleton, flushed with victory after the Battle of the Waxhaws in May of 1780. Above, his Green Horse cavalry slices through the broken ranks of colonial militia during the slaughter.

The 19th-century engraving at right recreates the horrors of the warfare in the Waxhaws during the later stages of the Revolution. Young Andrew Jackson (center foreground) stands by helplessly as enemy troops burn and pillage a settlement.

When a paper did arrive, people came from miles around to have the news read to them. By the time Andrew Jackson was nine years old, he was being chosen "public reader" in the Waxhaws as often as any grown man. Even some of his prosperous uncles must have looked up to him, for although they owned fertile fields and slaves and big houses, they could neither read nor write. Of all the news stories he read, he would always remember one that came on a summer day in 1776, a story about a declaration of independence passed by the Continental Congress meeting in Philadelphia. Andrew went over it beforehand and read it without a hitch, big words and all.

Although he may have been an indifferent scholar, he was bursting with energy for almost everything else. He loved the most active sports—high jumping, wrestling, foot racing. He would accept any dare and take any risk. While he was too light to be a good wrestler, he never quit trying. "I could throw him three times out of four but he would never stay throwed," a former classmate recalled years later. "He was dead game even then, and never would give up." But along with this fighting spirit there went a terrible temper and an inability to take a joke on himself. These weaknesses—for weaknesses they would certainly be considered in most men—would mark his early career. Once when he was with a group of friends they handed him a musket into which they had secretly crammed an extra-large powder charge. When he fired it, the kick knocked him sprawling. The enjoyment of the joke died at once as Jackson jumped to his feet, eyes blazing, and said, "By God, if one of you laughs, I'll kill him."

Young Andrew had hardly passed his eighth birthday when the Revolution began with the skirmishes at Concord and Lexington in Massachusetts. During its first years, the war hardly touched the Waxhaws except when a local boy left home to enlist in the Continental army, or when bitterness erupted between neighbors, caused by the continued loyalty of many people to King George III. Then, in 1780, the American General Benjamin Lincoln was trapped in Charleston by the British and forced to surrender with his entire army. This was one of the worst disasters of the war for the Americans, and gave all of South Carolina to the redcoats.

For the Jacksons, the bitter news of the defeat was preceded by tragic personal news. The oldest of the three sons, Hugh, had died in the campaign against the British. Hugh, only sixteen, had been sick and was under orders to stay in camp, but he took part in the fighting around Charleston anyway. He died from sunstroke and exhaustion, which were just as deadly as enemy bullets.

In May, 1780, the war came to the Waxhaws. Tories—Americans who remained faithful to the king—became bolder after the defeat of General Lin-

The tide of war in the South began to turn as Francis Marion took up Tarleton's challenge. Known as the "Swamp Fox," Marion specialized in hit-and-run raids on British outposts and lines of communication. On horseback, second from left, he is shown rafting across South Carolina's Pee Dee River with his men.

Captured in April, 1781, Andrew Jackson defiantly refused to clean an English officer's boots. The enraged officer dealt him and his brother (right) painful saber wounds, and then marched them off to prison.

coln. As American militia forces prepared to defend the region, into their midst, without warning, rode the cavalry legion of Lieutenant Colonel Banastre Tarleton. The Britisher caught the American force completely off guard and shattered it. Tarleton ordered his men to ignore cries of surrender and to continue killing; what had begun as a battle ended as a massacre. From then on, the cavalry leader was known as "Butcher" Tarleton.

That day was the blackest of the war for the people of the Waxhaws.

Andrew Jackson and his brother Robert went with their mother to the local church to help care for their frightfully wounded neighbors.

The patriots' cause grew worse. General Horatio Gates came south to try to patch up the wreckage left by the American disaster at Charleston. He immediately led his army to defeat at the hands of General Charles Cornwallis at Camden, only about forty miles south of the heart of the Waxhaws. The routed colonials fled as fast as they could, but their commander outdistanced them all. Now both Carolinas lay open and almost unprotected. Butcher Tarleton came riding back through the Waxhaws again, and the Tories rose up bolder than ever. Men were killed in savage and desperate battles in which every soldier on both sides was an American. In the South, the Revolution was truly a civil war.

Andrew Jackson was only four months past his thirteenth birthday when he joined the patriot forces after Tarleton's first raid through the Waxhaws. At first he did nothing more than carry messages. Later he joined in the skirmishing which found neighbor fighting neighbor, with small British forces often present to help the Tories. In one minor action, after their band was surprised by a British cavalry patrol, the two Jackson boys hurried to the house of a relative for refuge. The next morning they were surprised and taken prisoner, betrayed by a Tory neighbor.

The pair was hauled before the officer in command, and that arrogant young Englishman ordered them to clean his boots. Andrew was only fourteen and undoubtedly frightened. But he refused to clean the boots, and said he expected treatment proper to a prisoner of war. Moreover, considering his blazing temper, his refusal was probably neither polite nor tactful. In any event, the officer struck the boy with his saber, a blow that might well have killed him if he had not put up his arm to take its force. His left hand was cut to the bone, and a deep gash on his head left him with a scar the rest of his life. Then, without warning, the brutal officer also swung at Robert and wounded him badly.

The brothers were marched forty miles to a prison camp at Camden, South Carolina, and thrown into a stockade with 250 other patriots. Their wounds had not been treated, and in the camp there were no medicines, no beds, no blankets. The only food was stale bread once a day.

While they were there Nathanael Greene, who had replaced the disgraced General Gates, advanced on Camden. In full sight of young Jackson—who had whittled a peephole through a plank of the stockade—the Battle of Hobkirk's Hill was fought. It was the cruelest of disappointments. The American army was winning until one of Greene's commanders handled his forces badly at a critical moment; the American flank was turned and the advance was turned into a retreat.

An even worse misfortune struck within the stockade when smallpox spread among the prisoners. Both Jackson boys caught the disease. Then, when the future seemed completely without hope, their mother appeared. An exchange of prisoners had been arranged, and she had come to see that her sons were included in it, and to take them home. Robert, so weak that he had to be held in the saddle, rode one of the two horses Elizabeth Jackson brought. Mrs. Jackson rode the other while Andrew, suffering from the still-unhealed saber cuts as well as smallpox and lack of food, walked the forty miles to the Waxhaws.

Perhaps Elizabeth Jackson could have gotten her two boys home safely except for a cold, drenching rain that made their desperate condition worse. Robert died within two days, and for weeks there seemed hardly a shred of hope that Andrew would live. His mother nursed him until he was finally out of danger, but she could not remain until his recovery was complete —which would take months—for there were others who needed her help. It must have hurt her deeply to leave him, still sick and only a weak bundle of skin and bones, but she had a strong sense of duty toward her friends and neighbors from the Waxhaws who were imprisoned by the British.

The redcoats had retreated to Charleston, where captured patriots were crowded aboard prison ships in the harbor. Elizabeth Jackson made the 160-mile trip with two other ladies of strong will. They found the Waxhaws men, but while caring for the sick among them, Mrs. Jackson was struck down by "ship fever" (probably cholera). With other victims of the disease she was buried in an unmarked grave in an open field outside Charleston. When Andrew received the news, he was handed a small bundle containing his mother's spare clothes. "I felt utterly alone and tried to recall her last words to me," he said years later of that melancholy day.

The British remained in the port of Charleston for fourteen months after they had left the rest of the Carolinas, and a number of Charlestonians had taken refuge in the Waxhaws until they could return home. Andrew, always ready for fun and excitement, fell in with some young blades from the city who passed the time with horse racing, gambling, drinking, and cockfighting. When Charleston was liberated and they went home, Andrew did not have enough money to follow them.

Then, perhaps with unfortunate timing, his grandfather in Ireland died. The estate of three or four hundred pounds sterling (a goodly sum in those days) all went to Andrew as the surviving member of his family. This legacy could have modernized his father's farm, which now belonged to him, or it could have started him in a business of his own. Instead, he took it and set out for Charleston to visit some of his high-living friends and to experience the excitement of the big city.

In Charleston he had little luck with dice and worse luck betting on horses. In a remarkably short time his inheritance was gone, and he had no money left to pay the landlord at the inn where he was staying. While Andrew was pondering what to do, he happened on a dice game; before long, in desperation, he bet his horse against two hundred dollars on a single roll of the dice. He won, refused to gamble on another toss of the dice, paid his landlord, and rode out of Charleston.

He was a schoolteacher in the Wax-

*American artist John Trumbull drew this scene of
his countrymen starving aboard the British prison
ship* Jersey *during the Revolution. Authorities esti-
mated that the ship usually contained at least
1,000 prisoners crammed into her rotting holds;
deaths from disease and hunger averaged six a day.*

After the Revolution, the orphaned Andrew Jackson hurried to Charleston for a taste of city life. This gay gathering of militia officers and merchants was typical of pleasure-loving Charleston. One gentleman, labeled number 5, seems unaware that he has lost his wig to the waggish colonel in the foreground.

haws for a year or so, proving that a man did not need much education—or spelling ability—to be a teacher in those days. Then, at the end of 1784, when he was still in his seventeenth year, Jackson left the Waxhaws forever and headed north on his horse.

On Christmas Eve he was in the village of Salisbury, North Carolina, staying at an inn known as the Rowan House. Mr. Rowan's tavern had a reputation as a lively place at any time of year; at Christmas it was especially cheery and bustling, with holiday celebrators coming and going, toasting each other before the yellow flames dancing in the big fireplaces. In such an atmosphere Salisbury seemed to be just what Jackson was looking for, and he asked Spruce Macay, the leading lawyer in the village, if he could study law under him. Macay was agreeable.

There were no law schools then; a youth who wanted to become a lawyer simply "read law" with an established attorney until he was able to pass his bar examination. It was fortunate for Andrew that the road to becoming a lawyer was not too difficult, since he seems to have been too busy having fun to spend much time studying. Years later he was still remembered by a local man as "the most roaring, rollicking, game-cocking, horse-racing, card-playing, mischievous fellow, that ever lived in Salisbury . . . the head of all the rowdies hereabouts . . . more in the stable than in the office."

After two years Andrew left the boisterous atmosphere of Salisbury to attach himself to another lawyer for six months, then passed his bar examinations to become a lawyer in his own right. He probably practiced law for a year in and around Martinsville, North Carolina, although nothing is known for sure. Not only are the records of that time gone, but Martinsville itself has disappeared from the map.

At that time, North Carolina extended much farther west than it does today. Pioneers had established settlements on the western slopes of the Appalachian Mountains; beyond them civilization gave way to wilderness except for a colony planted by hardy frontiersmen much farther west on the Cumberland River in what is now Tennessee. The chief settlement was called Nashville. Here was the wild west of the day, two hundred miles beyond the settled frontier, reached through forestlands full of hostile Indians.

John McNairy, who had been Jackson's fellow law student and companion in mischief in Salisbury, had been elected a Superior Court judge for this remote Cumberland River settlement. Now, returning east for a visit, he described to Andrew in vivid terms the opportunities awaiting an ambitious young man out beyond the mountains. When McNairy returned to Nashville in the spring of 1788, his good friend Andrew Jackson went with him.

Davy Crockett's Almanac. 1841

Wild, savage fights were common among the rough-and-ready backwoodsmen of the frontier. Few had heard of the gentleman's code, and they were notorious for their eye-gouging and nose-biting tactics.

2　Frontier Hothead

Andrew Jackson was only one person in the stream of pioneers heading west through the mountain passes toward Nashville. Most of them carried axes, and expected to swing them from sunup to sundown building homes and clearing forestland for crops. But not Andrew Jackson. His friend John McNairy, elected justice of the newly created Superior Court of the Western District of North Carolina, had appointed Jackson his public prosecutor. Andrew Jackson came across the mountains not with an axe in his hands but with a lawbook.

The new prosecutor was still a long way from Nashville when his hot temper flared. Judge McNairy had been directed by the state to pause on his journey and hold court at Jonesboro, even though it was not in his new district. Jackson, as prosecutor, had to present the state's arguments in each case.

In one such case he was opposed by a lawyer named Waightstill Avery, an elderly and much respected gentleman who actually went out of his way to be helpful to the grass-green Jackson. In defending one of his clients, Avery several times jokingly mentioned how often his young opponent quoted from a book on law by a man named Bacon. (Bacon's book was one that most inexperienced young lawyers depended upon a great deal.)

Prosecutor Jackson, whose skin was as thin as his temper was quick, grew red and angry. At last he tore a flyleaf from one of his books—legend says that it was the very book by Bacon that had caused the trouble—scribbled a challenge to a duel on it, and thrust it at Avery. There was nothing unusual in Jackson's action. The custom of dueling, carried on within an elaborate "code of honor," was left over from the ancient era of chivalry when men seized their weapons to obtain satisfaction for real or fancied insults.

Avery did not want to fight with this tall, thin, sandy-haired, sharp-nosed young man. He rather liked him, and had nothing to gain by exchanging shots with him. But Jackson insisted, and arrangements were made for a duel the next evening at sunset. Fortunately, men of good sense talked to Andrew Jackson in the meantime; when the signal to fire was given, both men shot harmlessly into the air and then shook hands.

Had Avery known that Jackson lacked a sense of humor, he would have let matters drop there. But he wanted the affair to end with a laugh. He handed over a package, saying he was afraid that if he had wounded Jackson seriously, there would have been no way of comforting him "without your beloved Bacon." Jackson opened the package to find not a lawbook but a side of smoked bacon. A laugh went up, then died away when it was realized that Jackson alone was not amused. The boy of the Waxhaws, who had been ready to kill anyone who laughed when he was knocked flat by an overcharged musket, still had not learned to take a joke on himself.

Jackson and McNairy moved on toward Nashville, joining the first party of settlers to pass over a new road to the Western District. There were almost two hundred miles of wild, unsettled country to pass through. The state of North Carolina sent a sixteen-man guard along for protection against hostile Cherokees, but it was Jackson who noticed one night that the hooting of an owl did not sound quite right. Suspecting that it was an Indian signal, he alerted the party. His warning put the camp in such a state of readiness that the Indians gave up any idea of attacking and melted away into the forest.

Jackson arrived at his destination on October 26, 1788. Autumn lay hazy and pleasant over the Cumberland Valley as he looked down on Nashville for the first time. He saw a log courthouse only eighteen feet square, a distillery, two taverns, two stores, and a number of cabins and rough shelters. It was not much, but it was twenty-one-year-old Andrew Jackson's hope for the future.

It promised to be a busy future. The courthouse was filthy, and its door sagged on its hinges, indicating how low respect for the law had fallen in this far western settlement. The big problem facing the court at the time McNairy and Jackson arrived was that people who owed money had banded together and simply refused to pay their debts. There was only one local lawyer, and he had taken their side; no one represented the men to whom the money was owed.

Judge McNairy began to hold hearings in his Superior Court, and Prosecutor Jackson took vigorous action on demands by creditors that money owed to them should be paid. The debtors suddenly found themselves taken into court and ordered to honor their debts. Enforcement of the court's orders fell to the prosecutor, who

Journeying westward in the early days of the nation was at best a hazardous adventure. The most difficult method was via one of the pitifully inadequate wilderness "roads" (above); whenever possible, pioneers preferred to travel by river flatboat (right). These eyewitness sketches, including the frontier woodcutting scene below, are the work of an artist and part-time gun inventor named Joshua Shaw.

soon proved he was not to be tampered with. When a debtor attempted to bully him, Jackson said nothing; instead, he picked up a stick of wood and knocked the man flat. Respect for the law was quickly restored in Nashville.

Andrew Jackson took lodgings at the farm of the Widow Donelson, about ten miles out of town. Ten miles on horseback each way was a long ride, but it was awkward for Jackson to stay in either of the Nashville taverns because a number of the men he had hauled into court were living there. More important, the Donelsons were a large and influential family in the Cumberland country, and Jackson wanted to be on good terms with important people in the community who might help his career.

One of the members of Widow Donelson's household was her married daughter, Rachel Donelson Robards, home from Kentucky because of a quarrel with her husband. Lewis Robards, an intensely jealous person, had become angry with his wife for talking to another man, although the conversation was so harmless that even Robards' mother took Rachel's side. Yet Robards was more miserable without Rachel than with her, and came to Nashville to beg forgiveness. They made up their quarrel but were hardly back in Kentucky before they were quarreling again, and Rachel sent a message to her family asking them to come and get her. Instead of going themselves, her brothers sent Andrew Jackson to see that their sister got home safely through a country still not free of hostile Indians.

This was a mistake because soon Robards would sue for divorce, charging that his wife had "eloped" with Andrew. But for the moment nothing happened. Jackson delivered the pretty Mrs. Robards to her family. He had long since moved out of the Donelson's house and taken up lodgings elsewhere so that there would be no gossip. In fact, much of the time he was out of Nashville entirely, for Judge McNairy's court was a circuit court which traveled from settlement to settlement, trying whatever cases were waiting for it.

The next time Robards showed up, begging Rachel to return home again, he made menacing remarks about Jackson. Jackson's response was to go to Robards and threaten to cut off his ears with a knife. This was no help to poor Rachel, who did not want to go back to her jealous husband. She learned of a party of traders about to go by flatboat down the Cumberland, Ohio, and Mississippi rivers to Natchez in present-day Mississippi; to get away from her troubles Rachel made up her mind to go along.

The man in charge of the expedition refused to be responsible for a woman's safety on such a dangerous trip, and he suggested that Andrew join the group. By this time Jackson was more than a little interested in the lively, dark-eyed Rachel Robards,

and very concerned about her safety. He agreed to go along. The long trip was made safely, and after he had delivered her to friends in Natchez, he returned overland to Nashville by the shorter but far more dangerous Natchez Trace. On his arrival, he was startled to find that Robards had sued for divorce.

Divorce was very unusual in those days, so rare that it could be granted only by a state legislature. Robards had asked for a divorce, but the legislature had not given him one; it had only granted him permission, in December, 1790, to have the courts consider his complaints. The legislature would then give him a divorce if the reasons for it were good enough. As a lawyer, Jackson should have found out the real situation. But he

Cherokees were a constant menace to the Tennessee pioneers. This engraving shows an Indian raid on a settlement in 1796.

did not. Thinking the divorce was final, he set out again over the long trail to Natchez to tell Rachel. The news shocked and saddened her, even though her life with her husband had been unhappy.

But now she was free, and these two people, both twenty-four years old, were in love. In Natchez, in August of 1791, they were married. Jackson owned some land and a modest log house nearby, where they spent their honeymoon. Then they returned to Nashville, and he bought a small plantation named Poplar Grove on the Cumberland River.

His law work was hard on both of

31

them, for it kept him away from home
much of the time. While the tide of
settlers was making the area some-
what more civilized than when Jackson first arrived, the country was still
wild and dangerous. He was forced to
cross rivers in flood and had narrow
escapes from hostile Indians; when
caught in rain or snow, he had to
make what cold comfort he could on
the trail without shelter.

As for Rachel, she had to take
over the work of managing the plantation when her husband was gone,
and she did it well. She was always
helping neighbors, and frequently was
called out of bed in the middle of
the night to take care of a sick slave.
(Jackson was a slaveowner all his life
and never saw anything wrong with
slavery.) Rachel loved children and
always had nephews and nieces swarm-
ing around her, but she never had a
child of her own.

Both Andrew and Rachel looked
forward to the time when he could
settle down to being a country gentleman, riding over his fields, directing the planting and the harvest,
breeding race horses and running
them against the best his neighbors
could produce. For Rachel, it would
be enough just to have her husband
beside her in front of the fire in the
evening, perhaps talking, or perhaps
just quietly sitting and smoking their
pipes (for Rachel smoked a pipe; Andrew would fill and light it for her).

In December of 1793, Jackson
learned with deep shock that Lewis

As this 19th-century painting indicates, informal frontier justice was handed down in barns as often as in courthouses. "I several times saw a large can of cyder brought in from a neighboring tavern, and handed around amongst the jury," wrote a rural judge.

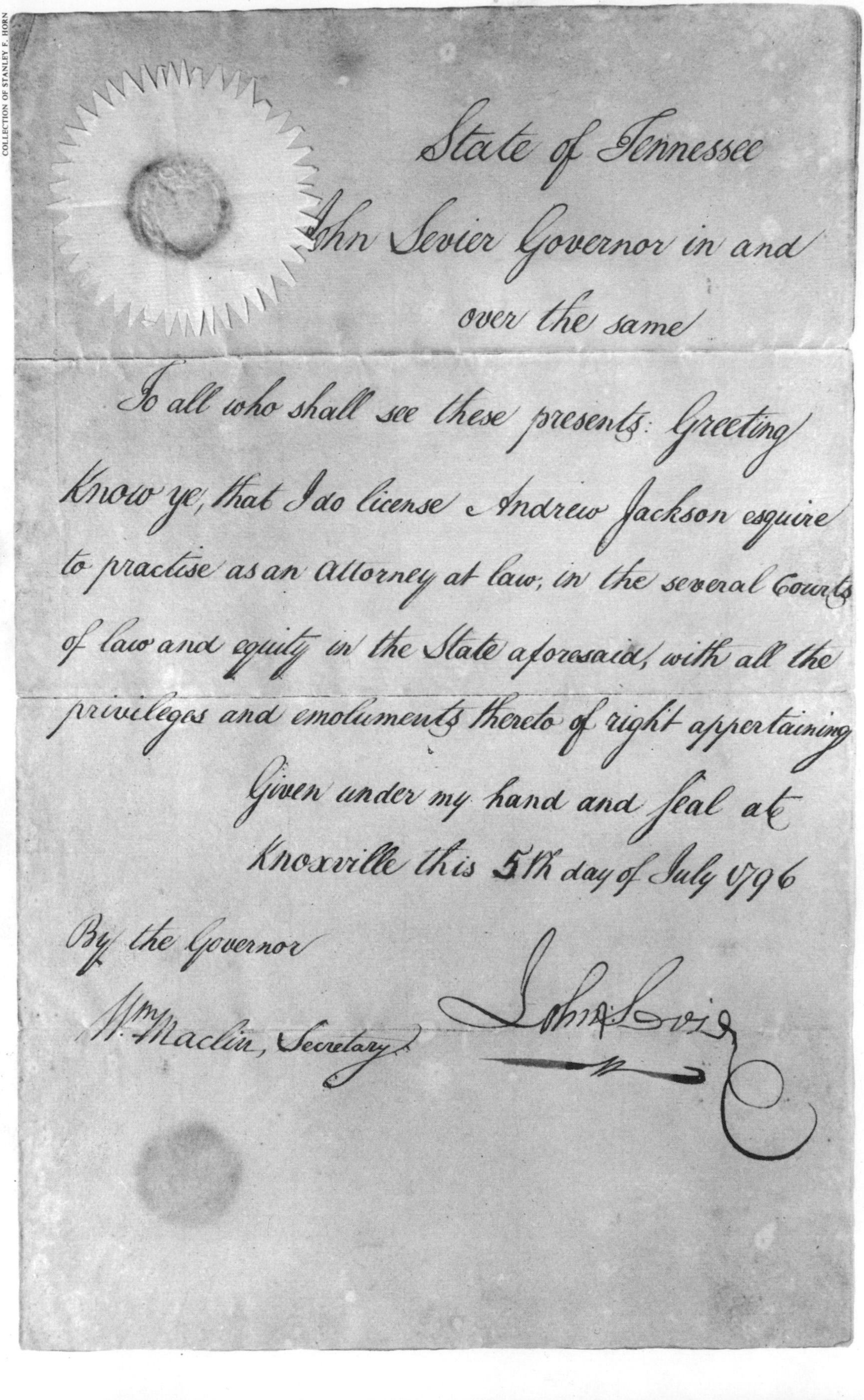

State of Tennessee

John Sevier Governor in and

over the same

To all who shall see these presents: Greeting

Know ye, that I do license Andrew Jackson esquire

to practise as an Attorney at law, in the several Courts

of law and equity in the State aforesaid, with all the

privileges and emoluments thereto of right appertaining

Given under my hand and seal at

Knoxville this 5th day of July 1796

By the Governor

Wm Maclin, Secretary

John Sevier

Robards had been granted his divorce only three months earlier. That meant Andrew and Rachel had been married for two years while she was still another man's wife—and so they had not been legally married at all. Jackson at once married Rachel again, and this time there was no doubt about the legality of the ceremony. Then he cleaned, oiled, and put in perfect order a pair of dueling pistols; he placed them in their velvet-lined case, ready for any man who made an insulting remark about the marriage. Twice he was to use them.

There were other things to keep Jackson busy besides the law and decisions about when to plant cotton or whether to buy a new slave. He was interested in military matters and he was soon judge advocate—the military legal officer—of the county militia. And there was always the Indian problem.

The Cherokees had already given up much of their territory to the whites and were fighting now because settlers were moving in and taking away land that, by treaty, was to belong to the Indians "as long as waters flow." On this point Andrew Jackson was a typical frontiersman: he thought that Indians had no right to any land that white settlers wanted, regardless of treaties, and never in his life did he change his view.

Jackson was an excellent farmer, and raised some of the best cotton, corn, and wheat in the region. His affairs were prosperous enough so

A law license (left) signed by Governor John Sevier was issued to Andrew Jackson when Tennessee became a state in 1796. Before a year had passed, the two men were bitter enemies.

Those honoring the dueling code were not supposed to fight with their fists, but frontier feuds often collapsed into street brawls (right). Jackson himself engaged in one such free-for-all.

Davy Crockett's Almanac, 1841

This early view of Natchez is a rare landscape painting by John Audubon, more famous for his pictures of wildlife. Not until 1798, seven years after Jackson's marriage there, was the bustling Mississippi River town ceded to America by Spain.

that he bought a better plantation for himself and Rachel, a place called Hunter's Hill. Things were looking bright for the Western District, too, as settlers continued to pour in. A special census showed that the territory had more than the 60,000 inhabitants needed to become a state. Jackson was a delegate to the convention called to write a constitution for the new state, and he is said to have suggested that it be called Tennessee— derived from Tinnase, the name of an early Cherokee chief.

Tennessee was entitled to one member in the national House of Representatives, and Jackson was elected its first congressman. He arrived in Philadelphia, then the national capital, in December of 1796.

Congressman Jackson did only two things in two years that were noticed at all. Soon after his arrival, he refused to vote in favor of sending to George Washington, just completing his eight years as President, a message thanking him for his services. Jackson had several complaints against Washington—foremost that the President had actually tried to enforce treaties by keeping settlers out of land set aside for the Indians. Jackson earned further attention by obtaining approval of his bill to have the government pay the entire cost of an expedition against the Cherokees that Tennessee citizens had undertaken some years earlier—even though the secretary of war had said that the campaign was neither necessary nor justified.

At the end of his term, Jackson refused to run for re-election. Within a short time, however, one of the two Tennessee senators was expelled for playing a part in a land fraud, and Jackson was appointed to take his place. Once again he rode to Philadelphia. But his service in the Senate was even less notable than his term in the House. Jackson was not a man for debate but for action. After a year he resigned and came home to Tennessee, and was appointed a justice of the state Superior Court.

He was a good judge, in a day when justice on the frontier was often handled in a free and easy manner. The central idea of his instructions to juries before they went out to reach their verdict was always the same: "Do what is right between these parties. That is what the law always means." It was a good rule to follow.

Jackson was now thirty-one years old and fast gaining a following in Tennessee. He was widely respected as a judge and as an advocate of western expansion—with the support of the Federal government and at the expense of the Indians. It was inevitable that his growing reputation would bring him into conflict with leading political figures in the state; this, plus his hot temper, meant that Jackson could not escape making enemies. His most prominent foe was John Sevier, governor of Tennessee, hero of the Battle of King's Mountain during the Revolution, and leader of thirty or more expeditions against the

The slanderous abuse hurled at Rachel Jackson by her husband's ene-
mies deeply hurt the retiring, soft-spoken woman. As proof of his devo-
tion, Andrew carried this miniature locket portrait for thirty years.

Horse fanciers of a backwoods settlement, as drawn by William T. Ranney during the 19th century, haggle over the price of a possible money winner.

Indians. He and Jackson became bitter political opponents, and a clash was bound to occur.

It finally came in 1803, as Sevier made a speech in Knoxville to the people who had helped elect him governor for the fourth time. He was talking on the steps of the courthouse where Justice Jackson had just completed the day's session. There were other doors Jackson could have used, but he marched out of the one behind Sevier, who was speaking of his services to the state. Jackson broke in to say that he also had performed great public services. Sevier's retort was made in a loud voice: "Services? I know of no great service you have rendered the country except taking a trip to Natchez with another man's wife!"

Jackson, in a white fury, rushed at Sevier with his heavy walking stick upraised; the governor drew an old saber he wore when making political speeches. There was scuffling, some pistol shots, and a bystander was slightly wounded before the two men were surrounded by their supporters and prevented from doing any real damage. Jackson at once sent Sevier a challenge to a duel. Sevier ignored it for several days until Jackson published a notice in the Knoxville newspaper calling him ". . . a base coward and poltroon. He will basely insult, but has not the courage to repair."

Sevier could not ignore this, and

the duel took place across the border in Kentucky. Sevier and his party arrived late, and what happened next is uncertain. According to one story, Jackson dismounted and drew a pair of pistols, Sevier did the same, and the two of them stood daring each other like schoolboys with chips on their shoulders. Another account says that Sevier stepped on his sword as he dismounted, frightening his horse, which ran off with his pistols. All the accounts, no matter how different otherwise, agree that the pair was ridiculous. In the end, no shots were fired and no one was hurt.

In 1804 Jackson had to resign his position as judge when his financial affairs went sour. He had loaned sums of money to a friend who was then unable to pay him back. Hunter's Hill was sold, and Jackson moved into a simpler plantation, one called the Hermitage. There he and Rachel lived in a stout log cabin.

But despite his unhappy financial situation, there were certain things he would not give up, and one of them was horse racing. He managed to find $1,500 to buy a horse named Truxton, then raised $5,000 more to bet on him in a race against a horse of great reputation named Greyhound. The race aroused terrific excitement, and much land, money, and scores of horses were wagered on the result. Jackson used every bit of his knowledge of horses in training Truxton, and the horse won handily.

Jackson had money now to pay off

some of his debts. He also gained a reputation as an expert on horseflesh, which meant a great deal to him. His horses reflected his own fighting spirit. On one occasion he matched Truxton against a very fast horse named Ploughboy for a purse of $3,000. Ploughboy's backers called off the race once when their horse became lame; another match was arranged, but Truxton strained a thigh muscle two days before the contest. Jackson decided to run him anyway.

To win, a horse had to take two out of three heats of two miles each. Truxton, despite his lame leg, took the lead at once in the first heat and held it all the way. But it was a dear-bought victory. Truxton's hind leg was worse, and a front leg had also gone lame. It did not seem possible that he could last the two miles of the

The first Hermitage was a group of cabins, but here Jackson entertained such men as Aaron Burr and President James Monroe.

41

second heat. Yet he not only jumped out in front almost at once, but was sixty yards ahead of Ploughboy at the finish. Jackson's reputation as a trainer of horses rose even higher.

A deadlier kind of contest, however, was on Jackson's mind at this time. A young man named Charles Dickinson had made some slighting remarks in public about Rachel Jackson's divorce and remarriage. Although Dickinson apologized to Jackson and said that his remarks were the result of too much whiskey, he was soon heard to repeat the same things. Dickinson was a young blade who enjoyed hanging around the Nashville taverns with his friends; he was well-liked and not a troublemaker at heart. He was also considered the best pistol shot in the state of Tennessee, and Jackson was convinced that his enemies were using Dickinson to force him into a fight to get rid of him.

The affair quickly developed into a bitter quarrel, with challenges given and accepted. In most duels, both men usually felt that honor was satisfied even when their shots went wide of the mark, and very often both duelists purposely shot into the air or the ground. But this time both men meant to shoot to kill. Dickinson was a crack shot—he could level and fire his pistol instantly, without appearing to take aim, and put the bullet through a bull's-eye. Jackson was neither a fast nor even an especially good shot; he knew that Dickinson would hit him first, and he hoped only to stay on his feet long enough to fire back.

The two men took their stations and indicated that they were ready. At the signal "Fire!" Dickinson shot at once without seeming to aim. A tiny puff of dust came from Jackson's coat and his hand went up to his chest, but Dickinson thought he had missed completely. He was so aghast that he took a step away from his mark and had to be warned back by Jackson's second who, by the code of dueling, would have shot him down otherwise.

Then, as Dickinson stood waiting helplessly, Jackson took careful aim and fired. His enemy slumped to the ground. Only after Dickinson was borne away did Jackson's friends discover that the young marksman's aim had been straight and true. Blood was streaming down Andrew Jackson's side. His tall, lanky body and his loose-fitting coat had misled Dickinson enough so that the ball had just missed the heart but had come so close that the doctors did not dare probe for it. Jackson carried it in his body until he died.

Dickinson, suffering terribly, lived only until evening. As for Jackson, although he had escaped death by less than an inch, there had never been any doubt in his mind that he was going to shoot down Dickinson. He was sure that his fighting spirit would have kept him on his feet as long as necessary. "I would have hit him," he said, "if he had shot me through the brain."

Rather unsettled after his dueling fiasco, John Sevier was comforted by a dream in which, he wrote, his dead father told him that Jackson was a "wicked base man, and a very improper person for a judge."

The Creek Indian uprising in the South during the War of 1812 was encouraged by both the British and the Spanish. Here, militiamen launch a raid against a Creek village near Alabama's Tallapoosa River.

3   Old Hickory

Nashville is far from the Atlantic coast, and a century and a half ago news usually traveled slowly over the rough roads across the mountains. But it was no ordinary news that was made on June 18, 1812. A courier galloped into the settlement after having traveled 860 miles in nine days to bring word that the country was at war with Great Britain.

The message was not a complete surprise; brash Westerners, convinced that British agents were stirring up the Indians along the frontier, were vehemently in favor of such a war, just as trade-minded New Englanders were violently opposed to it.

Andrew Jackson was now general of a division of 2,500 Tennessee militia. He won the position not by showing great military ability; he was elected to it by the officers of the division, beating his old enemy, John Sevier, by one vote. This was the usual method of choosing militia officers, and it produced some terrible misfits. In Andrew Jackson's case, however, it worked out well.

General Jackson immediately offered his division, ready for duty, to President James Madison. Nothing happened. An American army was badly defeated at Detroit, and American forces accomplished little elsewhere, but still the Tennessee division received no orders. It appeared that the administration in Washington wanted to avoid having anything to do with this outspoken political opponent from Tennessee.

But there was a back door into the war. The government in Washington called on the governor of Tennessee for 1,500 men to serve in an expedition against English forces in Florida, and the governor asked Jackson to take command of the state's troops. He would not be the top commander in the campaign, he was told; instead, he would serve under General James Wilkinson. This was a bitter blow to Jackson, but he replied that he was ready to serve his country in any way he could. The governor appointed him a major general of volunteers.

The militiamen began to arrive

KNOXVILLE BLOCKHOUSE
1795

The settlers of Knoxville, Tennessee, erected this blockhouse about 1793 as a defense against marauding Indians. That year Jackson himself was ambushed near the fort by Cherokees seeking revenge for the loss of their land.

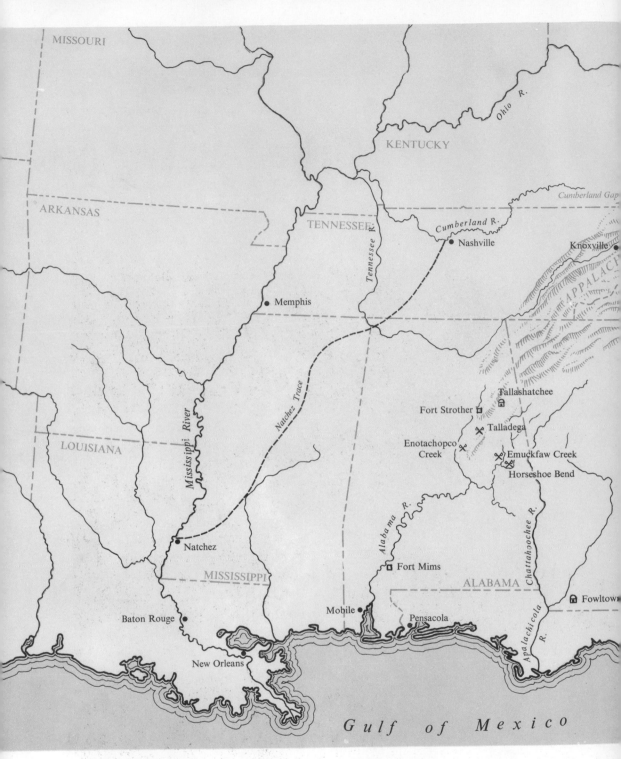

Shown here is the battleground in which Andrew Jackson carved his military career—from his youthful exploits in the Carolinas and his relentless pursuit of Indians in Alabama and Florida to his successful campaign against the British along the Gulf of Mexico in the War of 1812.

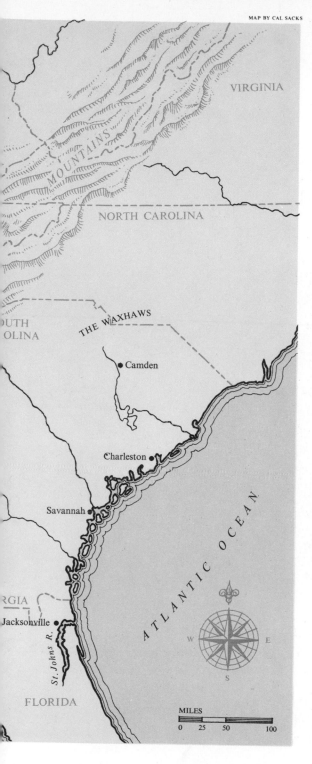

VIRGINIA

MOUNTAINS

NORTH CAROLINA

SOUTH CAROLINA

THE WAXHAWS

• Camden

Charleston •

Savannah •

ATLANTIC OCEAN

GEORGIA

Jacksonville •

St. Johns R.

FLORIDA

MILES

0   25   50   100

during the coldest spell of December weather Nashville had seen in years. General Jackson worked long hours —occasionally going all night without sleep—seeing that his men were kept warm enough and provided with rations, and taking care of the thousand details of organizing a force that by now had grown to more than 2,000 men. On January 7, 1813, the expedition was on its way. The main force went on flatboats down the Cumberland, Ohio, and Mississippi rivers to Natchez; the cavalry went by land over the Natchez Trace.

But when Natchez was reached, Jackson received orders telling him to wait there for further instructions. Waiting was a hard thing for a man of Jackson's temper, and when news came that another American army had been defeated in Canada, he asked to be sent north with his men. There was no answer to his request. Then, after more waiting, an abrupt message came from the War Department saying that the plans to invade Florida had been called off. General Jackson's Tennessee volunteers, no longer needed, were to be dismissed immediately from the service.

Jackson replied that he could not obey an order to dismiss his troops eight hundred miles from their homes without any pay, food, or transportation for the sick. He began to suspect that this was all part of a scheme

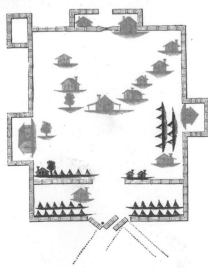

When a force of 1,000 Creeks descended on Alabama's Fort Mims in 1813, they found it ripe for the taking. The fort's commanding officer knew little of military tactics, and his troops lacked discipline. When the Indians charged, he discovered that the stockade gate could not be shut; the result was a massacre. At left is a plan of the fort.

to get rid of him, and he was right. General Wilkinson in New Orleans believed that if the young Tennessee volunteers were dismissed so far from home, they would soon be so badly in need of food and a place to sleep that they would gladly join the regular army. Thus, Wilkinson would get Jackson's division but not its troublesome general.

Jackson had no intention of letting his enemies get away with such a plan. He used his own money to buy wagons to carry the sickest men; the less ill were put on horses, including Jackson's own. The general himself went on foot. As they proceeded, building bridges across streams and chopping out a trail for the wagons, Jackson was everywhere, seemingly tireless. One of his men remarked, after the general had passed, "He's tough as hickory." To frontiersmen, who learned from long hours of swinging axes the exact hardness of every kind of wood, hickory was about the toughest thing they knew. And so Andrew Jackson was "Hickory" and then "Old Hickory," and the name stayed with him all his life.

As soon as he was home again, Jackson was once more writing letters to Washington, asking for a military command of his own. While he waited, his hot temper flared again and got him into another nasty fight.

One of his staunchest admirers during this period was a young lawyer and rising politician named Thomas Hart Benton, who had been with him on the fruitless expedition to Natchez. While Benton was away on a trip to Washington, his younger brother, Jesse, challenged a Nashville man named William Carroll to a duel for complicated and rather silly reasons. Carroll had also been on the Natchez expedition, and he asked his former commanding officer to be his second. Jackson reluctantly accepted the duty only after his attempts to settle the matter peaceably had failed.

The duel itself made history of sorts. Jesse Benton fired first and missed, then ducked to present a smaller target—whereupon Carroll shot him in the seat of the pants. It was undoubtedly a painful wound, but one that earned Jesse a great many laughs and no sympathy whatsoever.

When Thomas Benton returned from Washington and learned about the affair, his friendship with Jackson turned sour quickly. He wrote a letter to Old Hickory, telling him that it was poor judgment for a man of his position "to be conducting a duel about nothing between young men who had no harm against each other." Busybodies and troublemakers kept after both men, carrying gossip and false stories back and forth and raising the temperature of the quarrel. At last Jackson announced that he would horsewhip the older Benton the next time he saw him.

His opportunity came several weeks later, in September of 1814, when both men were in Nashville. Tom Benton was accompanied by his brother,

Jesse; with Jackson were John Coffee, the leader of his cavalry in the Natchez expedition and in many battles to come, and Stockley Hays, one of Rachel's swarm of young nephews. The Bentons, each carrying two pistols, were standing in the doorway of their hotel when Jackson and Coffee walked by. Jackson carried a pistol and a riding whip. Seeing the brothers, he raised the whip to strike as he rushed at Tom Benton, shouting, "Now defend yourself, you damned rascal!"

Benton reached for one of his pistols, but Jackson already had his own pistol out and poked against Benton's chest. Benton backed slowly through the doorway and down a hallway in the hotel, with Jackson following step by step, pistol still against his enemy's chest. Jesse Benton had also slipped inside, and as the two men went by a door, he fired, hitting Jackson in the shoulder. Jackson's pistol went off as he pitched forward, his bullet just missing Tom Benton; Benton, at last managing to get his own guns out, shot twice as Andrew sagged to the floor. But the excitement spoiled his aim, and he missed with both guns. A bystander stepped forward and shielded the bleeding Jackson when Jesse tried to shoot him again with his second pistol.

By now Coffee and Hays had come running down the hallway. Coffee, in the lead, shot at Tom Benton and missed. Then he tried to brain him with his empty gun (like the others'

Most of the men who joined state militia companies in the 1800's cared little for military discipline. Whenever drills were attempted, the results were usually as chaotic as in the scene above. William Sidney Mount sketched the militiamen at ease below.

pistols, his was a single-shot weapon). Benton retreated hastily, backed into a stairwell, and tumbled down out of the battlefield. Hays, who had a sword cane, came at Jesse Benton and made a thrust to run him through; the point struck a button and the blade snapped off. Jesse poked his pistol at Hays and pulled the trigger. But except for the first shot of the fight that had hit Andrew Jackson, no weapon that day seemed to have the power to do harm, and young Benton's gun failed to fire.

The battle ended there, and the Bentons withdrew from the scene. Jackson was very badly injured. Blood poured from his shoulder in a frightening stream, and for a time not one of the doctors in Nashville could stop it. They said that the arm would have to be amputated to save the general's life, but Jackson refused to allow it. The arm was saved, although Jesse Benton's pistol ball remained in it as a souvenir of the incident.

While Old Hickory lay in bed, still ill and weak, word came that the Creek Indians were on the warpath and had massacred some five hundred persons at Fort Mims in present-day Alabama, then part of the Mississippi Territory. Fort Mims was far south, near the Florida border, but Tennesseans, like all frontier people, became highly excited when Indians anywhere went on the warpath. They began raising an army to fight the Creeks, and they came to ask advice of their military expert, General Andrew Jackson.

The thought of action was medicine to Old Hickory. Rather than offer advice, he made an announcement. Although still too weak to get up, not only would he command the expedition against the Indians in person, but he would be ready to march against them in nine days.

He was true to his promise. He was shaky and pale, his arm was in a sling, and he moved with pain, but he was up and about and in command. Burly John Coffee, who had stood with him against the Benton brothers, had moved on ahead with his mounted troops to scout the Creek country. The Creeks were led by an unusual chief whose Indian name was Red Eagle but who had a better claim to his English name, William Weatherford, for he was seven-eighths white.

General Jackson moved south with his infantry to join Coffee. Supplies were to be delivered by a civilian contractor, but the teamsters could not bring their loaded wagons through the difficult country as fast as Jackson was pushing his men. When food began to run low, Old Hickory took stock of the situation and announced that he would push forward even if it were necessary to eat acorns.

They marched through deep forest where axemen had to chop out a way for the army to advance. In the shadowy woods, Creek scouts glided along beside the army, reporting its every movement. Yet, it was not the Indians who struck first. Jackson had directed his men to fortify their camp and to settle down for a rest when he learned

*Jackson's tough and reliable lieutenant, John Coffee,
responded to his promotion to brigadier general by
routing the Creeks at the Battle of Tallushatchee.*

that the Creek village of Tallushatchee was only twelve miles away. There were about two hundred of Weatherford's warriors in the village; Jackson sent a thousand men against it. One of them was a young man named Davy Crockett. "We shot them like dogs," Crockett said afterward.

Scouts reported that Weatherford and a thousand men were attacking the Creek village of Talladega, about thirty miles away, whose people had refused to join the rebellion. As an object lesson to his supporters, Weatherford had to punish the village; it was equally important for Jackson to show that he could and would protect those who remained at peace with the whites. He set out at once even though ill with dysentery and in considerable pain.

As the army neared Talladega, Jackson formed his men into a line of battle with the two ends curving forward. Not an enemy brave was to be seen. As the troops came closer, however, the loyal Talladega Creeks behind their fortifications pointed frantically toward a line of thick woods along a stream. Jackson sent a detachment of cavalry in that direction. When the horsemen neared the woods, Weatherford's hidden warriors revealed themselves with a volley of musket fire and charged screaming toward the soldiers. The cavalry retreated, drawing the pursuing Indians toward Jackson's infantry. The curving ends of the battle line now moved in and joined, trapping the braves within a circle of troops which poured gunfire into them from all sides.

The Indians fought bravely and at last forced one detachment of whites to give way. The Creeks poured through the break in the circle and escaped, leaving three hundred dead. Fifteen of Jackson's men were killed.

General Jackson returned to his base, which had been named Fort Strother, only to find that the supplies he had been waiting for so long still had not arrived. He held his men in camp as long as he could, giving the best of the remaining food to the sick, allowing no favors for himself or his officers. He was now in constant agony from dysentery, which had grown so much worse that it left his stomach weakened for the rest of his life. At last, with the men half-starving and on the verge of mutiny, Jackson was forced to begin the march home.

Only a few miles from the fort, they met the long-awaited supply train with its herd of beef cattle and wagonloads of food. The army camped on the spot and had a huge meal. Yet when Jackson gave the order to march back to Fort Strother, the men stood sullenly where they were, and one company started moving toward home. Jackson galloped his horse in front of the company and snatched a musket from a soldier. He leveled the weapon at the mutinous men, and his blue eyes were cold as he announced he would kill the first man who took another step toward Tennessee. After a tense minute, the would-be muti-

KENDALL, *Life of General A. Jackson,* 1843

Jackson (right) threatens to open fire on a detachment of his men attempting mutiny during the Creek campaign in 1813. Most of these troops left anyway at the end of their enlistment period. This print is from a biography of Old Hickory by Amos Kendall, a key member of President Jackson's administration.

neers turned around and began moving the other way. Jackson handed the musket back to its owner, who remarked quietly, "Shucks, General, it couldn't shoot anyhow." Someone checked the gun; it was in such bad condition that it could not be fired.

But Old Hickory's problems were far from over. The enlistment period of most of the men ran out on December 10, 1813, and the majority refused to stay any longer. Jackson tried to get them to remain at least until he could get replacements, but they streamed away by the hundreds.

The replacements arrived none too soon. Only 130 veterans were left by the time the eight hundred recruits came into camp. The new men were almost completely untrained, but they were all Jackson had, and he took them out into Creek country almost at once. They got their first battle experience when the Indians attacked them early one morning in their camp along Emuckfaw Creek. The untried militia, with backbone supplied by the handful of veterans, fought the redmen to a standstill.

Two days later the Creeks made another surprise attack, this time while the army was crossing another stream with a jaw-breaking name, Enotachopco Creek. The Indians rushed out of ambush yelling hideously, and fell on the rear guard of the army just as it began to cross the creek. Jackson had prepared a plan in case something like this happened. To make it work, the rear section had to stop the In-

dians long enough to give the rest of the army time to recross the river above and below where the fighting was taking place, and catch the Creeks from both sides.

The rear guard, however, panicked and ran toward the river crossing in complete rout. Only one officer and a few troops stood fast and, for a time, held Weatherford's braves away from the men struggling in the stream, too fear-crazed even to defend themselves. While they held, Old Hickory galloped up, shouting orders, swearing at the fleeing men and ordering them back into the battle. The panic ended, men turned and fought, and the Creeks were stopped and then driven back.

Now fortune was running in Jackson's favor. Heavy reinforcements were sent to him, and near the end of March, 1814, with more than 2,000 men, he was ready at last to march against Weatherford's main stronghold. This was a spot called the Horseshoe Bend of the Tallapoosa. Here the Tallapoosa made a big loop, and in the land enclosed by the river the Creeks had built their village, sealing off the narrow land approach with log barricades. Inside the bend were some nine hundred warriors.

The log fortifications were assaulted and finally taken. The ground inside the bend was rough and brushy, and there the Creeks continued the battle until almost all of them were killed. They were brave men; twice Jackson called on them to surrender, but they refused and fought until they died.

Lavishly dressed William Mac-Intosh (left), a half-breed chief of the Creeks, fought for Jackson at Horseshoe Bend. Menewa (above) was MacIntosh's personal enemy and a commander of the rebellious Creeks. Selocta (below), also a Creek chief, served as Jackson's scout; his medal bears a portrait of President John Quincy Adams.

William Weatherford was driven to voluntary surrender by the suffering of his people. He is shown entering Jackson's tent to accept the terms of peace.

The bodies of more than eight hundred Indians lay on the ground or drifted away in the river. Jackson lost 49 killed, 157 wounded.

But Weatherford was not among the enemy dead; he had been elsewhere on the day of the battle. Jackson moved on, cursing his luck, and went into camp after scattering the few remaining Indians who opposed him. Then, while his army rested in camp, an Indian without weapons, his clothing ragged, presented himself to the general with the simple words, "I am Bill Weatherford."

The two talked in Jackson's tent, the white victor and the almost-white vanquished, who had chosen to be a Creek because his great-grandmother was one. Jackson refused to accept Weatherford as his prisoner because the chief had come in of his own free will. Weatherford made only one request. He asked Jackson to send for the women and children of the war party, "who have been driven to the woods without an ear of corn. They never did any harm. But kill me, if the white people want it done."

Jackson said he did not want to kill the chief, and promised that he would supply food to the women and children. Weatherford in turn promised he would talk to the remaining hostile Creeks and try to turn them toward peace. Then the two men shook hands, and the chief left the tent and walked past the encamped soldiers and disappeared into the forest. It was the last Jackson ever saw of him.

General Andrew Jackson was famous as the hero of New Orleans when he posed for this miniature portrait in 1819. The original, painted on ivory by Anna Peale, measures two and a half by three inches.

4 The Hero of New Orleans

General Jackson returned briefly to Nashville, to find himself being praised across the nation as one general who could win battles in a war that was producing disaster after disaster. Then once again he said good-by to Rachel and to Andrew Jackson, Jr.—for the childless couple had adopted a boy four years before, the new-born son of one of Rachel's sisters-in-law who was too weak to care for him.

The news was grim as Jackson moved south. Napoleon had been defeated in Europe; and Great Britain, which had treated the war with the United States as of secondary importance, could now concentrate her powerful army and navy against the Americans. Some of those forces had already arrived. They captured Washington and burned the Capitol and the White House; others seized or damaged many points on the New England coast. Jackson did not know about these northern attacks yet, but word did reach him that an enemy squadron was in the Gulf of Mexico.

He took his small army to Mobile on the Gulf, arriving there none too soon. Abandoned Fort Bowyer guarded the entrance to Mobile Bay; the force Jackson sent to repair and garrison it was just in time to drive off a British sea and land force that tried to batter its way into the bay.

With Mobile safe for the time being at least, Jackson turned his attention to Pensacola. This was a ticklish situation—or would have been for almost any other man. Pensacola was not very far down the coast from Mobile, but it was in Florida, and Florida belonged to Spain, and Spain was supposedly neutral in the war. Jackson knew, however, that there were British warships in Pensacola harbor and British troops in the town, making Spain's neutrality little more than a pretense. His orders from Washington did not give him permission to move against Spain, but he was not a man who needed permission when he felt

something needed doing. He marched on Pensacola with 3,000 men, arriving there in early November, 1814.

Dependable John Coffee and his homespun Tennessee cavalrymen were with Jackson again. Old Hickory ordered the troopers to make a great deal of noise on one side of the town to convince the defenders that an attack was coming from that direction. In the meantime, he quietly worked his way around to the opposite side. The trick worked: both the garrison troops in town and the seven British warships in the harbor shifted to fire in Coffee's direction. When Jackson struck, he met only light opposition. The Spanish defenders gave up quickly, and the British did not even attempt to fight, but blew up the chief fort they were holding, went aboard their ships, and sailed away.

Jackson continued to stay one jump ahead of his enemy. He hurried back to Mobile to strengthen further the defenses there, then went on to New Orleans, certain that that city would soon be the object of a major attack. Even as he and his army marched west from Mobile, a powerful British army at Jamaica, in the West Indies, was setting sail for New Orleans.

As soon as Jackson arrived, he set about trying to seal up the many ways an enemy might approach the city. New Orleans is built on low, wet ground, and the land gets much swampier toward the broad delta of the Mississippi about a hundred miles to the south. The country is laced with winding, sluggish waterways called bayous, and a man who knows well this country of big trees, slow water, and Spanish moss can get from the Gulf of Mexico to New Orleans through any number of back ways. There are also two great bays to the east, Lake Borgne and Lake Pontchartrain, which provide an avenue leading close to the city. And finally,

The destruction of Washington in August, 1814, by British Admiral George Cockburn (left, looking smug as the city burns), stood as a humiliating symbol of defeat for America. The invading English troops took particular pleasure in burning the White House, which was left a gutted ruin (right) after the attack.

CULVER PICTURES

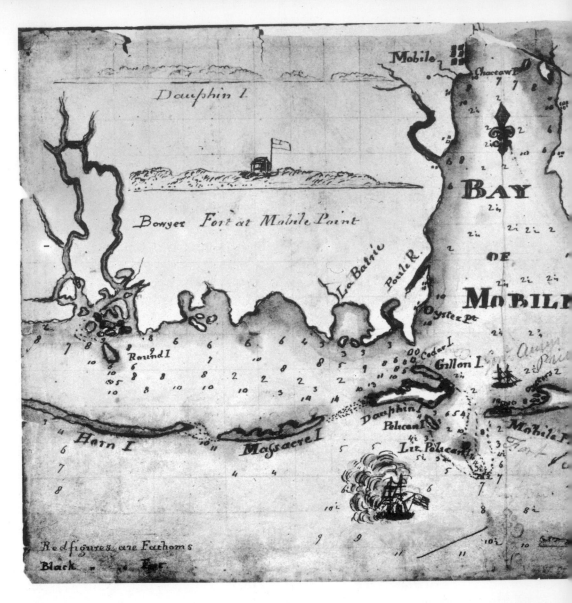

Mobile

Chactaw P.

Dauphin I.

BAY

Bowyer Fort at Mobile Point

La Batrie

Poule R.

OF

Oyster pt

MOBILE

Round I

Cedar I

Gillon I.

Dauphin I.

Pelican I.

Horn I

Massacre I

Lit. Pelican I.

Mobile P.

Fort

Red figures are Fathoms

Black " " Feet

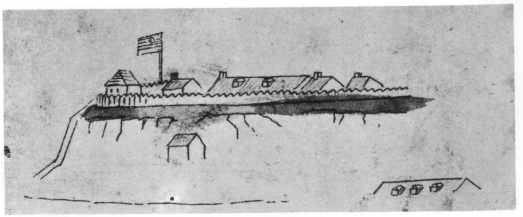

The 1818 map above, by a U.S. Navy officer, shows the strategic position of Fort Bowyer at the entrance to Mobile Bay. The fort, from which Jackson repelled a British attack, was built on the tip of Mobile Point, seen jutting into the bay at bottom center. The officer also sketched the American flag flying over Fort Barrancas (left) at Pensacola, Florida, another of Old Hickory's military conquests.

there is the Mississippi River itself.

Axemen were ordered out, and trees crashed across the bayous in a hundred places, forming jackstraw tangles through which it would take days for the enemy to cut his way. Fort St. Philip was manned and batteries of cannon set up to keep ships from coming up the Mississippi. On Lake Borgne, a fleet of five small gunboats began patrolling. Since the heavy English ships could not operate in these shallow waters, the gunboats seemed proof against an attack from that direction.

While he was taking care of these problems, Jackson was also trying to whip his strangely assorted collection of troops into an army. There were backwoodsmen from Tennessee, clerks, merchants, and bookkeepers from the business district of New Orleans, a battalion of freed slaves, and a smaller unit of Choctaw Indians. There were also many Frenchmen, veterans of Napoleon's armies who had fought the British many times before. And there was Jean Lafitte.

Lafitte was a pirate, but since he robbed only Spanish ships, he was considered in New Orleans to be more or less a gentleman. He and his brother Pierre, also a sea robber, tried to offer their services to help defend New Orleans. They had many good friends in the city who pleaded their cause, but Jackson refused to listen. He said angrily that he would have nothing to do with such "hellish banditti."

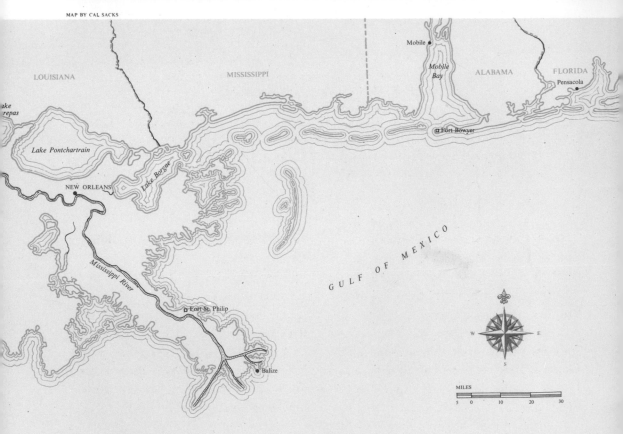

MAP BY CAL SACKS

LOUISIANA

MISSISSIPPI

ALABAMA

FLORIDA

Mobile •

Mobile Bay

Pensacola •

□ Fort Bowyer

Lake repas

Lake Pontchartrain

Lake Borgne

NEW ORLEANS •

Mississippi River

□ Fort St. Philip

• Balize

G U L F   O F   M E X I C O

W — E
S

MILES
5   0   10   20   30

Bargeloads of Tennessee troops (above) ride the slow current down the Mississippi to reinforce Jackson's patchwork army at New Orleans. The British threat to Mobile and Pensacola (map at left) had been thwarted without too much difficulty, but New Orleans lay open to attack from a number of directions. The Americans sealed off one route by guarding the narrow channel between Lake Borgne and Lake Pontchartrain. The British landed at the edge of Lake Borgne, proceeding toward the city by way of a bayou.

Jean Lafitte was not a man to be put off easily. He walked to the general's headquarters and asked to see the dragon in his own cave. No one but the two men ever knew what passed between them, but the soft-spoken pirate won his point, and General Jackson accepted his services. It was a wise decision on Old Hickory's part, for Lafitte's men would be of valuable assistance to him in the days ahead.

A strong British fleet carrying a large army was reported off the entrance to Lake Borgne, and then came the unhappy news that the little fleet of American gunboats had been mishandled and taken. What Jackson did not learn was that an enemy exploring party, searching for a water route

Britishers propel their barges into action against the American gunboat flotilla on Lake Borgne. The English sailors had rowed for a day and a half to join battle.

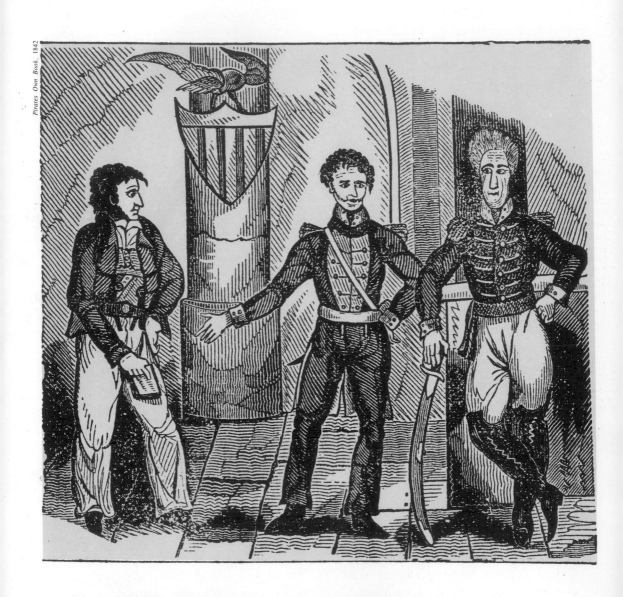

Veteran of Napoleon's army and confirmed pirate, Jean Lafitte wormed his way into American favor by rejecting a tempting British bribe. Awarded a pardon by the authorities, he played an important role in the defense of New Orleans. Lafitte (left) meets Louisiana's Governor Claiborne (center) and Jackson.

to New Orleans and finding bayou after bayou blocked with trees felled by the American axemen, had at last discovered one that had been completely overlooked by the defenders. It was named Bayou Bienvenue; soon soldiers in small boats were making their way up its waters to solid ground on the plantation of a family named Villeré, next to the Mississippi and about eight miles south of New Orleans.

General John Keane, who commanded this 2,000-man advance section, undoubtedly could have gone on and taken New Orleans without a fight. The American forces were too scattered to have opposed him. But prisoners told Keane that Jackson had twelve or fifteen thousand men (an outrageous lie), and Keane cautiously decided to wait until more troops came up to support him.

When the first British soldiers had arrived at the plantation, they took everyone there prisoner. But at the first opportunity Major Gabriel Villeré, the son of the owner, sprinted away from his captors, leaped a fence as bullets whistled around him, and headed up the river road for New Orleans and Jackson's headquarters. Old Hickory was shocked to learn that the enemy had approached without being detected, but he wasted no time wringing his hands over it. "By the Eternal, they shall not sleep on our soil!" he announced as soon as Major Villeré had finished his story. Then, turning to his aides, he declared,

"Gentlemen, the British are below; we must fight them tonight!"

Jackson immediately started rattling off orders as though this were what he had been planning all along. Units were sent hurrying to take up advance positions two miles away from the enemy, as yet unaware that the Americans had come. It was December 23, 1814, almost the shortest day of the year. At 6:30 P.M., in full darkness, John Coffee's troops began to work their way along the edge of a swamp to strike the British on the flank. At the same time, the American schooner *Carolina* silently drifted down the Mississippi and anchored opposite the British camp.

At 7:30 the *Carolina* opened fire with a crash of cannon. The British were thrown into complete confusion as the cannon balls tore into their camp, and Jackson allowed a half-hour for the bombardment so that they would think the schooner was their only foe. Then his infantry advanced, Coffee's men from the side and the main body of the army from the front, and the enemy was caught by surprise again. But these British soldiers were veterans of the Napoleonic Wars, and they did not panic. In the darkness it was often impossible to tell friend from foe; riflemen fired at the flashes of other rifles, and only rows of flickering tongues of flame marked out the opposing lines— or what lines there were in that confusion.

At nine o'clock the *Carolina* stopped

Mississippi

River.

Public Road.

Encampment
Sd Reg

B. McCarty's Plantation

Rodriguez Plantation. Maj

7th Regiment. Plauché's Battalion. Jacob's d. Savary's Corps. No.4 Regiment.

Camp   Jackson.

Powder Magazine.

Levee.

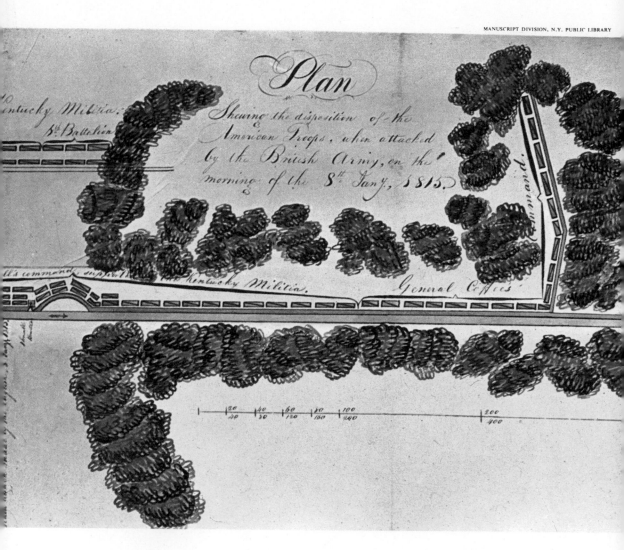

Plan

Shewing the disposition of the American Troops, when attacked by the British Army, on the morning of the 8th Jan.y, 1815.

Kentucky Militia: 5th Battalion

Kentucky Militia.

General Coffee's

The deployment of Jackson's troops along the Rodriguez Canal in the decisive New Orleans engagement is shown in the contemporary plan above. The American breastwork extended from the Mississippi River to John Coffee's position in a cypress swamp. As shown in the painting on pages 78–79, the main British thrusts were launched along the river bank and against Coffee's position. At the left is an engraving of the Villeré plantation, taken over by the enemy as a headquarters.

At the age of sixteen, Edward Pakenham was commissioned a captain in a British infantry regiment; seven months later he was a colonel. During the Napoleonic Wars, he continued to climb in rank until finally, at thirty-six, he led the British forces at New Orleans as a major general.

firing, and several hours afterward Jackson ordered his men to withdraw, planning to attack again when it was light enough for him to see what was happening. But by daylight many more British troops had come up, and Jackson, now badly outnumbered, began to entrench his position. Running from the river to a swamp three-quarters of a mile inland was a dry ditch called the Rodriguez Canal; about ninety feet behind the canal Jackson put his men to work throwing up earthen ramparts. If the British tried to move toward New Orleans, they would first have to break through this fortification.

Jackson's naval strength was doubled when the ship *Louisiana* joined the *Carolina*, and on the day after the battle the two vessels kept up a constant fire on the British positions. Cheers would have gone up in both camps that Christmas Eve if the men had known that a treaty of peace, ending the War of 1812, was being signed that very day at Ghent, in Belgium. But it would take many weeks for the speediest sailing ship to bring the news; many brave men were doomed to die needlessly as a result.

On Christmas Day, Major General the Honorable Sir Edward Pakenham arrived to take command of the British army. The thirty-six-year-old Pakenham had played an important role in the war in Europe. He was brave, able, and noted for his kind treatment of those he had conquered. A brother-in-law of the great Wellington, he was hopeful of making a greater military reputation for himself in the United States.

Pakenham at once had big guns, along with a furnace for heating shot, brought through the bayous from the fleet off Lake Borgne, seventy miles away. On December 27, the guns opened fire on the *Carolina*, which had been causing so much trouble. Cannon balls heated to glowing red in the furnace were soon lodging in the schooner and starting fires; her seamen did their best to save her, but they finally had to abandon ship. A few minutes later the *Carolina* blew up with a tremendous explosion that rained burning wood a mile away.

The British guns then shifted to the *Louisiana*, which by now had her sails up. The breeze was too faint to move her, so the crew went ashore with tow lines, and the *Louisiana* began to move slowly even as a red-hot ball plowed across her deck. With the sailors pulling mightily on their cables, she was towed to safety.

The American lines grew stronger

OVERLEAF: *Hyacinthe Laclotte, an engineer in the Louisiana militia, painted the Battle of New Orleans from his eyewitness sketches. Pakenham's main attack is shown in progress against the American left. In the foreground a British column tries to scale the fortifications with ladders; bunched together, the Englishmen are easy targets for Jackson's sharpshooters. At the far left, an American mortar duels with British artillery.*

COLLECTION OF EDGAR WILLIAM AND BERNICE CHRYSLER GARBISCH

each hour. Hundreds of new troops arrived, more mud was piled on the ramparts, and cannon were dragged into place. Two guns were served by men from the destroyed *Carolina*. As dawn began to light the sky, a band of red-shirted, mud-spattered men arrived breathless from New Orleans and took over a cannon that had been put in place during the night. They were Jean Lafitte's pirates, men who knew how to handle heavy guns.

At full light on December 28 the British opened fire with artillery and salvos of rockets. Half the Americans had never been in battle before, and even the veterans found the rockets, with their trails of fire and their strange sounds, especially terrifying. Officers moved along the ramparts calming them, and there was no panic. Then the enemy infantry appeared, their uniforms of red, green, gray, and Scottish tartan splendid in the first rays of the morning sun. The *Louisiana* moved far enough downstream to hit the enemy soldiers with her broadsides; then the artillerymen on the ramparts started firing.

When the British infantry came within range of the sharpshooting riflemen manning the earthworks, they began to falter and take cover behind fences or ruined plantation buildings or in shallow ditches. General Pakenham at last had to admit defeat and order his soldiers back. The British had lost the second battle for New Orleans.

The Americans continued to strengthen their earthworks. More cannon were put in place, and several big guns were set up on the opposite bank of the Mississippi to fire across the river into the enemy camp. Jackson, as usual, was everywhere, often going all night without sleep (on one occasion he got no sleep for three days and nights in a row). This would have been a strain on a man in perfect health, and Old Hickory should have been in a sick bed. For months he had been suffering from dysentery. Sometimes the pain was so agonizing that he had to bend over with his chest pressed against something until the attack passed. During much of the time he was in New Orleans the only food his weak stomach would accept was boiled rice. Only his tremendous will kept him going.

With backbreaking effort, the British brought up more guns from the fleet. These were put in position as quietly as possible by crews working all night on New Year's Eve. When morning came, the dumbfounded Americans found a wicked-looking line of cannon facing them less than half a mile away. The enemy guns opened fire at once, wrecking first one American cannon, then a second and a third, then blowing up a powder cart. But the American guns soon answered, and the artillery duel raged through the morning. By noon the enemy fire began to weaken, and soon all of Pakenham's guns were silenced, their carriages splintered, their emplacements battered into shapeless

In this print, dating from about 1819, Edward Pakenham lies dying amidst the carnage of his once-grand
army. The general was struck by a load of grapeshot as he rallied his faltering men. At battle's end
500 Englishmen who had saved themselves by feigning
death rose like ghosts from the field to surrender.

heaps of mud, many of their crews dead. Once more General Pakenham had failed to break through the American line.

Pakenham realized that he could not get through Jackson's fortifications without help. His next plan was to land part of his force on the opposite side of the Mississippi to seize the American guns there. These were to be turned against Jackson's troops behind the ramparts at the same time that the British infantry marched against their front. A canal was widened so that boats from the fleet could be hauled to the river for the crossing,

and the attack was scheduled for January 8, 1815.

On the appointed date the sky barely showed a pale light in the east when a rocket burst over the British positions. It was the signal for the advance to begin. But things did not go well. The force crossing the river was several hours late in getting started, it was short of boats, and the current carried it a mile downstream. As a result, it got into action too late to help the main attack.

Nothing had gone quite right with the main attack, either. It was to have been made in the dark to avoid

ATTENTION.

THE committee of arrangement is authorised to state to the citizens of Nashville and its vicinity, that GENERAL JACKSON will arrive at Nashville on Monday next. Messrs. *G. M Deaderick* and *Thomas Claiborne*, members of the committee, are deputed to meet GENERAL JACKSON, with such other citizens as may be desirous of accompanying them, at Franklin on Sunday evening, and the next day to escort him from thence to Nashville.—Messrs. *James Jackson* and *John Childress*, two other members of the committee, will meet the *General* at some convenient place, a few miles south of Nashville on Monday, and in conjunction with the Franklin escort, conduct him into town. The citizens of the town and neighborhood, are *all* respectfully invited to join them on horseback, at 10 o'clock monday morning, on the public square.
May 12, 1815.

Jackson's victory at New Orleans unleashed a wave of patriotism that engulfed the entire nation, particularly the border regions. Typical of the new spirit is the 1815 cartoon at left, in which John Bull, traditional symbol of England, is hauled rudely out of the Louisiana swamp. The broadside above announces a homecoming parade for Old Hickory in Nashville.

the deadly American marksmanship, but there were exasperating delays. Jackson's men had no trouble seeing their targets. The enemy infantry came on in perfect alignment, as though on parade. The cannon tore great gaps in the oncoming ranks, tossing bodies about like sacks of grain. Still they moved forward until they were within rifle range; then the American ramparts became continuous sheets of flame. The enemy lines melted away.

General Pakenham dashed to the front to keep the faltering advance moving. His horse was killed under

him and his right arm shattered, but he mounted another horse and urged the men forward in a new advance. The British ranks were cut apart once more; a charge of grapeshot struck the general and his staff squarely, injuring Pakenham so severely that he died within a few minutes.

A handful of men reached the Rodriguez Canal, and a Major Wilkinson got as far as the top of the ramparts, only to fall mortally wounded into the arms of Kentucky soldiers. He died two hours later. A Lieutenant Lavack, however, managed to reach the top of the ramparts unhurt and called on the Americans in front of him to surrender. He was told to look behind him. He did, and was astounded, as he later described it, to find himself alone—the men he led "had vanished as if the earth had swallowed them up."

It had taken only about half an hour to shatter the British attack, although the American cannon fired for another hour before they silenced all the big guns of the enemy. However, all was not going so well on the opposite side of the river.

There the American forces were retreating upriver, spiking their guns to prevent the British from using them. Jackson feared that a spirited advance could keep right on moving up the river and take New Orleans. But General John Lambert, who had assumed command on Pakenham's death, did not have Jackson's warlike nature; he was shocked by the heaps of dead along the canal and called his forces back across the river.

The forces opposing each other along the Rodriguez Canal had been about equal at the beginning of the battle, some 5,000 on each side. The British losses that day were 2,057, of whom nearly three hundred were killed; many more of the wounded died in the next few days. The Americans lost eight killed and thirteen wounded on the ramparts. Counting the fighting on the other side of the river, their total casualties came to only thirteen killed and thirty-nine wounded. American forces have never won another such one-sided victory.

After ten days, the British slipped away quietly during the darkness, leaving tents standing, fires burning, and dummy sentries on duty so that it was late morning before the Americans discovered they were gone. Soon afterward Jackson took his own army back to New Orleans.

Rachel Jackson and Andrew, Jr. arrived by keelboat from Nashville to visit the general, whom they had not seen for seven months. Official word that a treaty of peace had been signed did not reach the city until March 13, more than two and a half months after the actual signing. Then military law was lifted, and New Orleans gave itself up to wild celebrating, with Jackson the lion of the hour. His volunteer soldiers were released and sent home. Then he, too, left, and by mid-May, 1815, was back at the Hermitage with Rachel and young Andrew.

Old Hickory was then forty-eight years old, at that moment the most popular and famous man in the nation. Most of that fame and popularity, which one day would bring him the Presidency of his country, was won in a battle fought after the War of 1812 was over, a battle that did not influence in the slightest degree the war's outcome.

A common exercise of folk artists of the 1800's was turning out idealized pictures of national heroes. General Jackson and his Lady *presumably depicts Andrew and Rachel celebrating the New Orleans victory.*

84

Generall Packson and his
Lady

At a ball given for Jackson in Washington in 1824, the guest of honor stands flanked by four future political enemies (left to right): John C. Calhoun, Daniel Webster, Henry Clay, and John Quincy Adams.

5 Road to the White House

After his return from New Orleans, Andrew Jackson spent five months at the Hermitage, months that were probably as pleasant as any in his life. With plenty of rest, his shattered health mended, and he was eager for action again. At last he was home with his wife and son; Andrew, Jr. was now almost six years old and the pride of the fierce warrior's heart. Old Hickory sold his cotton and tobacco crops for high prices and was completely out of debt for the first time in almost twenty years. And along with everything else, he had been asked to remain in the regular army at a high rank.

After the War of 1812, when the army was reduced in size, it was organized into a northern and a southern division, with a major general to head each. Jackson accepted command of the Division of the South and the rank of major general that went with it. It was a perfect job for the returned warrior. The pay was excellent, and the duties did not take up much of his time or energy. He was able to make the Hermitage his headquarters and spend many happy hours there. Whenever he did travel, men greeted the hero of the Battle of New Orleans by telling him that he should run for President when the next election came around. Jackson shrugged off such suggestions—he had no wish to be President, he insisted—but the talk grew louder and louder in the months that followed.

Events soon called General Jackson away from this pleasant existence and back to army command in the field. The problem began with the Seminole Indians on the border between Georgia and Spanish Florida. All the Seminole towns were in Florida except for one, a village called Fowltown, just on the Georgia side of the boundary. The Indians there were peaceful enough. Trouble came because they wanted to continue living where they had always lived, even though Jackson's 1814 treaty with the rebellious Creeks stated that Indians could not hold land in that part of Georgia. General Edmund Gaines,

Thomas Sully's heroic painting, for which the cover portrait was a study, mirrors Jackson as he was seen by the "common people."

commander of the troops along the border, decided that the Indians of Fowltown, peaceful or not, had violated the treaty and must be removed. Choosing the direct method, he attacked the village and chased the Indians out after a brisk battle.

The entire Seminole tribe rose in vengeful anger, launching raids against the settlements in Georgia. General Gaines received orders from Washington to punish the Indians, to pursue them across the border into Spanish Florida if necessary, but to stop short of attacking any Spanish post. Hampered by this last restriction, Gaines could only flounder bewildered through the almost pathless forests against a foe who could flee to a Spanish fort if threatened. On the day after Christmas, 1817, General Andrew Jackson was ordered to Florida to take over command of the campaign.

Jackson, as always, was a whirlwind of activity when there was something to be done. He rounded up a brigade of veterans of the Battle of New Orleans, swore them in, and started south. He had already sent off a letter to President James Monroe saying that the instructions given General Gaines about respecting Spanish rights made it impossible to win the campaign—American forces would have to go wherever their Indian enemies went. Jackson added that he had a simpler plan for solving the whole problem: just take Florida away from Spain. All the President had to do was to give him some hint "that the possession of the Floridas would be desirable . . . and in sixty days it will be accomplished." When President Monroe did not answer the letter and give the hint, Jackson decided his silence meant approval. A man like Andrew Jackson usually found reasons for doing what he wanted.

General Jackson and his brigade reached Fort Scott near the Florida border in early March, 1818, where almost 2,000 troops awaited them. He led them at once into the swamplands along Florida's Apalachicola River. When word was received that the Seminoles had gone to St. Marks to demand guns, he marched to the town, seized it, and accused the Spanish officer in command of helping the Indians. No Seminoles were found, but one prisoner was taken, a Scottish trader named Alexander Arbuthnot.

Arbuthnot was an old man of seventy with flowing white hair. He had been a trader among the Indians for many years, treated them fairly, and did his best to defend them against those who took advantage of them. Because he spoke out against the way the Indians were cheated by both Americans and Englishmen, he came to be looked upon as a suspicious character—few frontiersmen of that day thought that Indians had any rights which were worth respecting. Jackson spoke of Arbuthnot as "the noted Scotch villain" and ordered that he be held for trial.

ORDINANCE,

By Major General Andrew Jackson, Governor of the provinces of the Floridas, exercising the powers of the Captain General and of the Intendant of the Island of Cuba over the said provinces, and of the Governors of said provinces respectively.

Regulating the fees of Justices of the Peace.

It is ordained, That from and after the date of this ordinance, the Justices of the Peace within the province of West Florida, shall be entitled to receive for their respective services the respective sums hereinafter mentioned, that is to say—

For celebrating the rites of matrimony, two dollars.

For a state warrant, fifty cents.

For a search warrant, fifty cents.

For a peace warrant, fifty cents.
For a warrant in civil cases, fifty cents.

For a judgment, fifty cents.
For an attachment, and taking bond and affidavit, one dollar.
Taking examination, fifty cents.
Transcript of record, when required, twenty-five cents.
Taking depositions, fifty cents.
Proceeding on appeal and bond therein, one dollar.
Mittimus on recognizance, fifty cents.

Execution on judgment, fifty cents.

And if any justice of the peace shall ask, demand, receive or exact from any person, any other or greater sum than by this ordinance he shall be entitled to demand and receive, upon conviction thereof in any court having cognizance thereof, he shall be fined in a sum not exceeding two hundred dollars, and shall lose his office.

Done at Pensacola, this 21st day of August, 1821.

ANDREW JACKSON,

By the Governor:
GEO. WALTON,
Secretary of West Florida.

Andres Jackson, Mayor General y Gobernador de las provincias de las Floridas, exerciendo en ellas la autoridad y poder que existian en el Capitan-General é Intendente de la Isla de Cuba sobre dichas provincias, y en los Gobernadores que eran de las mismas.

Para el reglamento de los Jueces de Paz.

Se manda, que desde la fecha de esta órden, serán acreedores los Jueces de Paz de esta provincia de la Florida occidental, por sus servicios respectivos, á las sumas asignadas, y es como sigue—

Por la celebracion del matrimonio, dos pesos.
Por un acto de Alguazil Mayor, quatro reales.
Por un acto que da autoridad para buscar, quatro reales.
Por un acto de Juez de Paz, quatro reales.
Por un acto en los casos civiles, quatro reales.
Por una sentencia, quatro reales.
Por una execucion, fianza y declaracion, un peso.
Por un exâmen, quatro reales.
Por una copia de protocolos, quando se pida, dos reales.
Por cada declaracion, quatro reales.
Por el procedimiento sobre apelacion y fianza, un peso.
Por un auto de *mittimus* sobre reconocimiento, quatro reales.
Por una execucion sobre sentencia, quatro reales.

Y si qualquier Juez de Paz pidiere, recibiere, ó exigiere de qualquier persona, otras ó mayores sumas de las ya designadas en esta órden, en caso de hallarse reo por sentencia de qualquier corte que tenga conocimiento de dicha ofensa, será condenado á una multa que no excederá de doscientos pesos, con pérdida de su empleo.

Dada en Panzacola, el dia 21 de Agosto, de 1821.

The general next hurried his forces to the village of the Seminole chief Boleck, more than a hundred miles away through swamps and tangled forests, hoping to catch the main enemy force by surprise. But he found the village deserted. His fury at being fooled grew hotter when he learned that the Indians had slipped away after being warned by a message from Arbuthnot that Jackson's force was too strong for them to fight.

That night the army's sentries captured Robert Ambrister, an ex-lieutenant of the British marines, who had come to Boleck's village not knowing it was held by the Americans. Ambrister was accused of helping the Indians wage war against the United States and was taken back to St. Marks to stand trial along with Arbuthnot.

Arbuthnot was charged before a military court with "exciting" the Indians to war, acting as a spy, and giving aid to the enemy. There is no doubt that the old trader was sympathetic to the Indians. He had warned Chief Boleck to retreat rather than to fight, and this alone was enough to condemn him in Jackson's eyes. Arbuthnot admitted that he had sold gunpowder to the Seminoles, but only enough, he said, for their hunting.

As governor of Florida, one of Old Hickory's official acts was to set the fees of justices of the peace. An 1821 handbill printed in English and Spanish announces new rates, including one of $2 for a marriage ceremony.

He readily confessed to treating the Indians as friends and human beings. The court decided that he was guilty of all the charges except spying, and sentenced him to be hanged.

As for Ambrister, he was charged with taking command of Indians at war with the United States. There was proof that he had obtained arms for the Seminoles and had actually sent one party of warriors to oppose the American advance. The Englishman admitted that he was guilty and asked the court to show mercy, but he was sentenced to die before a firing squad.

General Jackson was on his way again even before the two men had been put to death. Forgetting all about the Seminoles, he hurried west to Pensacola and, on May 24, seized it from the Spanish without a fight. Here, in the capital of Florida, he acted the part of a conqueror. Leaving one of his officers in charge as military governor, he headed for Tennessee, feeling that with Florida firmly under American control his work there was finished. There was anything but happiness in Washington when the news of Jackson's activities reached the city. The indignant Spanish Ambassador protested to President Monroe, who hastily called a cabinet meeting. Secretary of State John Quincy Adams alone defended Jackson's seizure of Florida; the other members of the cabinet strongly disapproved, and Secretary of War John C. Calhoun proposed that the general should be reprimanded. For a time President

Monroe was tempted to agree with Calhoun and let Jackson take the blame for everything, but Adams stood up stubbornly for the stormy general.

The President and others may have been concerned over the possible international effects of Jackson's raid, but the American people, as usual, approved Old Hickory's direct methods. More than anything else, the realization that the people supported Jackson gave new boldness to the President. The forts were returned to their Spanish officers, but Spain was warned bluntly that if she could not keep order in Florida she had better turn the territory over to someone who could. The next year Spain sold Florida to the United States for five million dollars.

At the Hermitage, Jackson once more occupied himself with being a planter. A new and handsome mansion was built to replace the log house that he and Rachel had moved into fifteen years before. The general told his friends that it was built to please Rachel, for he did not expect to spend many years there himself; he had returned sick and tired from Florida and was sure he did not have much time left to live.

In 1821 the long negotiations involved in drawing up the Florida treaty were finished at last, and President Monroe asked Jackson to become governor of the new territory. Old Hickory hesitated. Twice he had gone into Florida as a warrior; to be a governor seemed dull by comparison. Finally he agreed to supervise the transfer of Florida from Spain to the United States, and to govern there until it could be organized as a regular territory. Resigning from the army, he left Tennessee in the spring of 1821.

This time Rachel went with him. Although she had been in New Orleans once before, she was scandalized when they passed through the gay city. "Great Babylon is come up before me," she wrote in a letter home. "Oh, the wickedness, the idolatry of this place! Unspeakable riches and splendor!" At Montpelier, Alabama, where they made another stop, she was shocked again—no one there respected the Sabbath.

It would be too much to expect that Andrew Jackson would handle his new job without striking fire. He immediately plunged into an argument with the Spanish governor, Don José Callava, about who should make the first call on whom. (This matter of the first call was considered quite important in dealings between the representatives of nations.) Jackson waited outside Pensacola and wrote stiff letters asking Callava to call on him; the Spanish governor wrote smoother letters claiming that he was much too sick to call on Señor Jackson, but that he would be delighted to have the señor call on him. His patience quickly exhausted, Jackson went to pay the first visit.

In Pensacola's town square the flag

Kentucky's Henry Clay (top) broke with Jackson over the invasion of Florida and came to consider him the body and soul of despotism. Fiery John C. Calhoun (below) was also angered by the Florida venture, but the real basis of his hatred was Jackson's stand on states' rights. Old Hickory later admitted regret that he had neither shot Clay nor hanged Calhoun.

94

One cartoonist depicted the 1824 Presidential campaign as a foot race between John Quincy Adams (leading), William Crawford (second), and Jackson (third). Of the fourth candidate, a spectator asks, "How is Clay now," and is told, "Oh, dirt cheap."

As pugnacious before the camera as he was in politics, Missouri's Thomas Hart Benton was almost murdered on the floor of the Senate by a colleague after a particularly heated argument. Once an enemy of Jackson, Benton managed to smooth Old Hickory's ruffled pride, and they became loyal allies.

of Spain was hauled down, the American flag raised, and Jackson, in Pensacola for the third time, finally saw Florida become part of his own country. But there was still the slippery Don José Callava to deal with. The former governor stayed on to finish up the remaining business of his king. He argued for days that the cannon in the forts were not part of the deal and should be taken away by the Spaniards. He wanted to know who was to pay for the food of the Spanish soldiers on their short voyage to Cuba. He raised a hundred such points until Jackson wanted only to be rid of him.

Old Hickory finally exploded when he learned that the former governor was preparing to take certain public records out of Florida to help friends of his who were trying to cheat a woman out of her rightful inheritance. When Jackson sent his officers to obtain the records, Callava refused to see them. He said that Jackson had no right to the records, then that he did not understand English, and finally that he did not know what records everyone was talking about. For Jackson this was the last straw. He ordered Callava thrown into the city jail. The Spaniard was released the next day, and that was the end of the troubles with him; Don José Callava took the next ship out of Pensacola.

Very soon after the Callava incident, Old Hickory sent a letter to the President saying that he had organized things in Florida and was therefore quitting. He did not even wait for his successor to arrive, but climbed into his coach with Rachel and said good-by to Pensacola for the last time.

Although Jackson, now fifty-four years old, talked again of settling down at the Hermitage to spend the rest of his days as a gentleman-planter, a small group of his friends had other plans for him. Their ambition was nothing less than to make him President of the United States. It was a scheme with many practical difficulties—they had no political machine, and they would have little help from their candidate, who seemed to show no interest in the nation's highest office.

The plan went into operation in 1822, two years before the election. Jackson's supporters pulled enough political strings to have the Tennessee legislature nominate Old Hickory for President. (Before the days of nominating conventions, state assemblies proposed the Presidential candidates.) Jackson offered no encouragement except to say that, although he did not want to be President, it was an American's duty to serve if elected.

The next year, 1823, Jackson unexpectedly turned up in the United States Senate. His election came about through the complexities of Tennessee politics; Jackson was asked to run for office as the only way of preventing the election of an anti-Jackson man. Old Hickory reluctantly agreed to serve if he won, which he did easily.

In the Senate, Jackson came face-to-face with an old enemy for the first

Most of the riotous ingredients of an American election in the early 19th century are

depicted in John Lewis Krimmel's contemporary painting of voting day in Philadelphia.

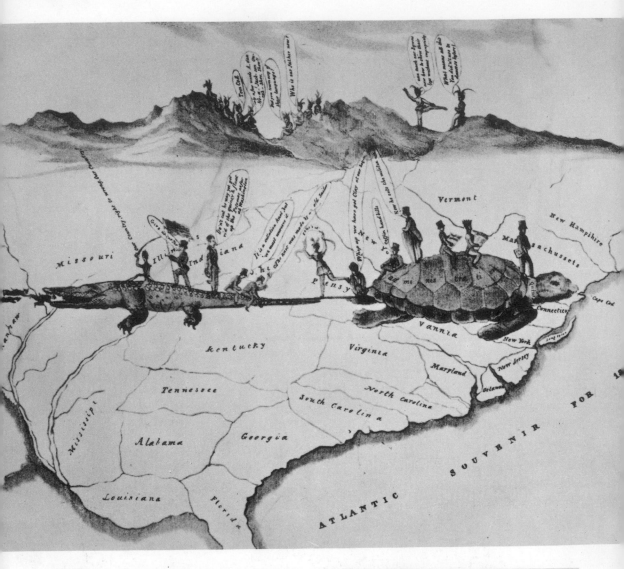

Some Account of some of the Bloody Deeds of
GEN. JACKSON.

Jacob Webb.   David Morrow.   John Harris.   Henry Lew.   David Hunt.   Edward Lindsey.

A brief account of the Execution of the Six Militia Men.

was the only one who betrayed feminine weakness. The awfulness of the occasion; his wife and nine children;

"MYSELF. I would not wish to die in "this way"—here his voice faltered, "and he passed the back of his right

his very words: "Colonel!"—the Colonel was close to him—"Colonel, I "am not killed, but I am sadly cut

taken humanity, failed to shoot him—but four balls had entered his body. "An Eye Witness" appeals to Col.

time since he had held a pistol at his chest ten years earlier. He and Thomas Hart Benton, senator from Missouri, were placed on the same committee. No sparks flew when they first met. Jackson merely made a few remarks about the business of the committee, and later Benton asked politely about Mrs. Jackson. The quarrel healed swiftly. Benton, in the days ahead, would be one of Jackson's firmest supporters. Jesse Benton, however, whose pistol ball was still lodged in Jackson's shoulder, never got over his hatred, and was bitter toward his brother for settling the quarrel.

Speaker of the House Henry Clay, Secretary of State John Quincy Adams, Secretary of the Treasury William Crawford, and Secretary of War John C. Calhoun were also nominated for President. All of them, like Jackson, were members of the political party started by Thomas Jefferson and called Republican, although it was actually the forerunner

The 1828 election was lampooned as a tug of war (left) between Adams' tortoise and Jackson's alligator. The famous "coffin handbill" (lower left) recalled the execution of mutinous soldiers, but it backfired; its author is shown below in a post-election cartoon staggering under the weight of Adams, Clay, and the coffins.

of today's Democratic party. Calhoun soon withdrew his name from the Presidential race to become the candidate for Vice President on both the Jackson and Adams tickets.

With all four Presidential candidates wearing the same party label, the average voter chose his man because of the region he came from and the economic group he seemed most in sympathy with. Crawford, who had most of the party leaders behind him, was eliminated as a serious contender when he suffered a paralytic stroke, although he refused to withdraw from the race. Adams, in general, was the businessman's candidate, and was strongest in the industrial East. Clay, a Kentuckian, had his best following in the booming West.

But Andrew Jackson was supported by the common people everywhere, and that support grew as the election neared. He did little campaigning himself, nor was it necessary. John Quincy Adams remarked that all the Jackson workers had to do to arouse enthusiasm was shout "8th of January and New Orleans!"

After election day, when the vote-counting was finished and the last returns reached Washington in mid-December of 1824, Andrew Jackson was well ahead of his opponents.

John Quincy Adams, the sixth President, was the son of the nation's second President, John Adams. Gilbert Stuart began this portrait, but painted only the head; it had to be completed later by Thomas Sully.

He had ninety-nine electoral votes; Adams had eighty-four; Crawford captured forty-one; and Clay had thirty-seven. But no one had received a majority, and the Constitution provided that in such cases the House of Representatives should decide among the top three. It seemed certain that Jackson would win.

In the House, each state cast a single vote when deciding a Presidential election. Since Jackson had carried eleven states in the national election, it was expected that the vote would go about the same way in the House. He needed the votes of only two other states to win a majority, and there seemed little doubt that he could get them.

But Henry Clay, who was out of the running, asked his friends to support Adams. When the House finished its vote, the result was thirteen states for Adams, seven for Jackson, and four for Crawford. Clay was appointed secretary of state by the new President soon afterward, leading to the charge that the two men had made an unsavory political deal.

Andrew Jackson felt that he had been cheated out of the Presidency, and he was fighting mad. In the 1824 campaign he had not been an eager candidate, but now he started working toward the 1828 election almost as soon as Adams had been inaugurated. The old Republican party of Jefferson now split into two wings. The followers of Adams called themselves the National Republicans. The

103

The people of a small town welcome President-elect Andrew Jackson as he pauses on the way to his inauguration in 1829. The first leg of his triumphal journey was by steamboat from the Hermitage to Pittsburgh, from where he went by coach to Washington.

"Jackson is to be President, and you will be HANGED," warned this cartoon, referring to the execution of Arbuthnot in Florida.

Jacksonians became known as Democratic Republicans, and later just as Democrats, the name the party bears to this day.

Jackson resigned from the Senate and was immediately nominated again for President by the Tennessee legislature. This time Adams and Jackson were the only candidates, and the campaign continued without pause for three years. Political principles were forgotten, and it sank to some of the lowest depths ever reached in any Presidential contest.

The Jackson forces harped on the "corrupt bargain" which they claimed had robbed their candidate of the Presidency and the people of their choice. At barbecues, veterans' reunions, fish fries, and other such gatherings, Jackson people sawed the air with their arms and reminded the crowds that it was brave Old Hickory who had saved them from the Indians and beaten the British at New Orleans.

The Adams forces told the country that Jackson was a man of bad habits who swore and played cards and gambled. They brought back to public memory all the deaths that could be laid at Jackson's door: Dickinson killed in a duel, Arbuthnot and Ambrister executed in Florida, six young militiamen court-martialed and shot for mutiny during the War of 1812. The matter of Jackson's marriage was raked up again, and one pro-Adams newspaper even invented a slanderous story about Jackson's parents.

Although President Adams did not personally take part in any of these gutter politics, Jackson held him responsible for dragging Rachel and their marriage into the campaign, and for other deliberate distortions of fact. He never forgave Adams; the President, he felt, could have put a stop to such methods if he had wanted to. The truth of the matter is that the campaign had gotten out of hand. Both candidates were honorable men, but their supporters had taken the bit in their teeth and run wild.

At any rate, Jackson had his revenge on election day. Adding the states of New York and Pennsylvania to his southern and western support, he received 178 electoral votes to 83 for Adams. John C. Calhoun won the Vice Presidency.

At the Hermitage, Rachel Jackson began making preparations to move to Washington as First Lady of the land. She was then sixty-one years old; she had grown heavy over the years, and time had afflicted her with a heart condition and other ailments. Apparently the bustle and excitement were too much of a strain, for on December 17, 1828, she was stricken with an agonizing heart attack. The doctors bled her, as they did for most ailments at that time, and the next morning most of her pain was gone.

For three days she improved. On the third night, Andrew and the doctors left her and went to sleep in nearby rooms. But Rachel was restless and had a maid help her to a chair by the open fire where she smoked her pipe. "I would rather be a doorkeeper in the house of God than live in that palace," she remarked. She had said the same thing on other occasions; by "that palace" she was referring to the White House.

Less than half an hour later she called out that she was fainting and fell into the maid's arms. She died soon after her husband and the doctors got to the room.

Rachel Jackson was buried in the garden of the Hermitage the day before Christmas. There was fear that her grieving husband might not be able to stand the shock of his loss, but the tough fiber that had given him the name Old Hickory was still there. On January 18, 1829, he visited her grave once more. Then he went down to the Hermitage's landing on the Cumberland River and boarded a steamboat which was to take him on the first stage of his trip to Washington.

Haunted by the specter of "King Andrew the First," Jackson's enemies began at once to fight against the spread of popular democracy, which they considered simply mob rule.

6 The People's President

Andrew Jackson was inaugurated as the seventh President of the United States on March 4, 1829. It was a sunny day, although patches of snow could still be seen on the great lawn in front of the Capitol. A huge crowd gathered to see the famous warrior take the oath of office, a crowd very different from those that had watched other inaugurations.

The majority were men in worn, often homespun clothing and scuffed boots—frontiersmen from Tennessee and Kentucky, backwoodsmen from Indiana and Michigan, hungry war veterans, a sprinkling of laborers and factory workers from New York and New England. Andrew Jackson had won the Presidency by appealing to the "common man"; now the common man had come to Washington to see the festivities.

Many of these men were also there because they wanted something from the new President. They had been jamming into the city for weeks, sleeping several to a bed in the hotels, or on the floor and on billiard tables when the beds were filled. Jackson's advisers had tried to shield him from this mob, but he felt he should shake hands with every tobacco-chewing backwoodsman who cornered him; these backwoodsmen, he said, represented the people who had elected him.

After the inauguration, when Jackson mounted his horse and rode down Pennsylvania Avenue toward the White House, his followers were far from ready to go home. They streamed along behind him, and did not stop at the gates or doors of the White House itself. The new President was to give a reception for members of Congress and high government officials and their wives; long tables bearing punch and food were set up in the East Room of the mansion.

The unruly crowd shoved its way inside. Men in muddy boots climbed on expensive brocade chairs to catch a glimpse of Old Hickory, and others elbowed and pushed through the mob to the food. China was broken, food

In this caricature, The President's Levee, or all creation going to the White House, *English satirist Robert Cruikshank poked fun at those who struggled for a glimpse of Old Hickory at the inaugural reception.*

trampled into the carpet, and clothing torn; elegantly dressed ladies were bumped and pushed about until some of them fainted. President Jackson, shoved against the wall, was protected by friends who linked arms and formed a barrier to keep his over-enthusiastic supporters from crushing him. Later they helped him escape, and he had to spend his first night as President in a hotel. It was hours before the last of the uninvited guests left the White House.

The scene at the reception seemed to justify the worst fears of conservatives, who concluded that the Republic was dead and that mob rule had taken over. They soon had something more to be concerned about when the President began to replace Adams men in government jobs with loyal Jackson men. The Jacksonians spoke of this as "reform," and to some extent it was; yet, at the same time, they were using government jobs to pay off political debts and to build a political machine. Commenting on this "reform," a senator remarked, "To the victor belongs the spoils." From that day on, the language of American politics had a new phrase—the "spoils system."

Some state political machines had been using the spoils system for years, but it was Jackson who introduced it on a national scale. Yet, it was never so widespread as tradition has made it, or as Jackson's enemies claimed. During his first year, when the move to replace officeholders who had supported Adams was at its height, only some 9 per cent of all the positions were filled by Jackson men. During Old Hickory's entire eight years in the White House, the total was about 20 per cent, or one in five. Nor did all these changes represent Adams men fired for no good reason. Many were normal replacements for those who had died or retired, and there were those who needed replacing because they were dishonest or incompetent.

To Jackson (and to most later Presidents) this system was both logical and desirable, for it brought into the administration men who were sympathetic to its policies. Trouble arose when a man's fitness to serve the government began to be measured by his faithfulness to a political party rather than by how well he could carry out his work. It was not until fifty years later that the enactment of Civil Service reforms began to curb the abuses of the spoils system.

In common with all strong Presidents, Jackson did not lean heavily on the advice of the department heads who formed his cabinet. Instead, he depended on a small group of

The opposition party set up a great hue and cry against Jackson's replacement of Federal officials with men loyal to himself. The spoils system, as it was branded, inspired this vicious cartoon showing the President as a winged demon dangling political plums before hungry office-seekers.

Peggy Eaton (above), looking prim and proper in Mathew Brady's daguerreotype, shocked Washington society with her supposedly shady reputation. As far as the President was concerned, however, she was the "smartest little woman in America." A different view was held by Old Hickory's niece and White House hostess, Emily Donelson (left). To her, Mrs. Eaton was a "source of great mortification."

friends who gathered regularly in the back rooms of the White House, and whom the opposition soon began calling the "Kitchen Cabinet." After 1831, however, when he reorganized his regular cabinet, he came to depend upon it more; Andrew Jackson had learned that the advice of amateurs at government was not always a sufficient guide for a President.

Almost from his first day in office, the President was involved in a battle he was unable to win but from which he was too stubborn to retreat. On this occasion the famous warrior was opposed by the ladies of Washington, and he found himself in hot water.

Jackson had appointed as secretary of war an old friend from Tennessee, John Eaton. Eaton had recently married a young lady named Margaret O'Neale Timberlake. What made fashionable Washington cluck and lift its eyebrows was that his bride had been the cause of a suicide and at least one challenge to a duel by the time she was fifteen, had been married at sixteen and widowed at twenty-nine, and had worked as a barmaid in her father's tavern.

Peggy Eaton's reputation outraged the ladies of Washington society, and they refused to call on her. Jackson, who seemed to think he could overcome society the way he defeated Indians, urged the unhappy members of his cabinet to call on the Eatons. But their wives refused, and there was nothing the angry President could do about it. Andrew Jackson

G. P. A. Healy painted Daniel Webster's great moment: his "Reply to Hayne," delivered in the Senate in January, 1830, denouncing the nullification theory as a dire threat to the Union.

Donelson, one of Rachel's nephews, was Jackson's personal secretary, and his wife, Emily, served as official hostess in the White House. The President ordered Emily to break the social boycott imposed on Mrs. Eaton. Although Emily loved the stubborn old man, she firmly refused, and as punishment the young couple was sent back to Tennessee for a year. Secretary of State Martin Van Buren was the only cabinet member to pay a call; he could well afford to do so, for he was a widower.

The whole affair would have been ridiculous had it not interfered with the running of the government. Jackson seemed prepared to fight on forever. "I would resign the Presidency sooner than desert my friend Eaton," he said when someone hinted that the secretary of war should resign. There is no telling how long the situation might have continued had not Van Buren acted. Realizing the affair was doing the administration no good, he brought everyone to their senses by resigning from the cabinet. Secre-

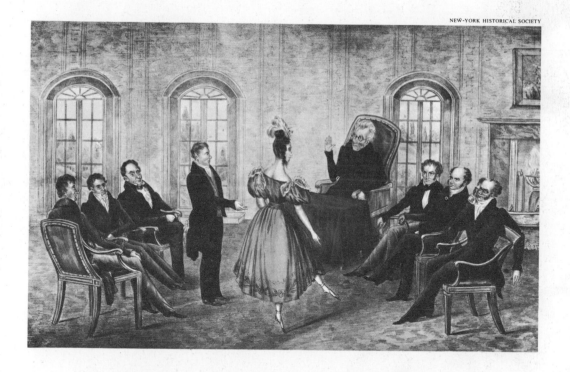

Throughout the nullification crisis, Jackson was harassed by trouble from every direction. His cabinet was embroiled in the Eaton affair, provoking a new flood of ridicule (above). The nullification and Peggy Eaton issues caused all but one cabinet member to resign; the cartoon at left compares this to rats leaving Old Hickory's crumbling house.

The nullification issue inspired this 1833 print, showing Calhoun and his friends climbing the steps of treason and civil war to attain their goal. Jackson (right) threatens them: "By the Eternal, I'll hang you all."

tary Eaton at last took the hint and did the same.

A considerably greater upheaval occurred when the President asked three of the remaining four cabinet members to resign, for quite a different reason. They were supporters of John C. Calhoun, and Jackson was no longer on good terms with his Vice President.

For one thing, he had just learned that during the days when Washington was in an uproar over his seizure of the Spanish forts in Florida and the execution of Arbuthnot and Ambrister, Calhoun had recommended to President Monroe that Jackson be reprimanded. Even stubborn Old Hickory could have swallowed this if Calhoun had not split with him on the most basic of issues —that of the powers of the Federal government.

While the President was being defeated by the ladies of Washington in his fight to have Peggy Eaton accepted socially, other and vastly more important matters were taking place. One of these, the great nullification controversy, struck at the very existence of the Union itself.

Calhoun was a leader of strong forces, mainly from the South, that held that a state had the right to nullify—simply refuse to enforce—any Federal law until it had been approved by three-quarters of the states. Any law not so approved, the nullifiers insisted, was unconstitutional. The issue was dramatized in January, 1830,

when Senators Daniel Webster of Massachusetts and Robert Hayne of South Carolina debated the powers of the Union and of the state governments. Hayne argued the case for strong states' rights and nullification, Webster the case for a strong Union. Webster's reply to Hayne, which lasted two days, is considered one of the most moving orations ever made in the Senate. "Liberty and Union, now and forever, one and inseparable," were his closing words.

After the debate, both sides waited for the President to take a stand, but Old Hickory carefully avoided choosing sides publicly. Then, on April 13, 1830, nullification leaders in Washington gave a Jefferson Day Dinner, and invited Andrew Jackson. Twenty-four prepared toasts were on the program, most expressing sentiments strongly in favor of states' rights and nullification. Jackson sat patiently through all twenty-four of them. As guest of honor, he would offer the first volunteer toast that followed. He had given a great deal of thought to the matter the night before, for he wanted to be sure that his few words said exactly what he meant.

Now the President stood up and waited for the room to be quiet. In the expectant hush, his words rang out: "Our Union: It must be preserved."

There was complete silence. Old Hickory had taken his stand, and it was not at all what the nullification forces had hoped for. Vice President

A prime issue of the 1832 election was the President's promise to destroy the Second Bank of the United States. It was, he said, a citadel of the aristocracy and a barrier to the advancement of the lower classes. Shown here is Jackson's plan as the opposition Whig party saw it —a vicious scheme to bleed the country of its wealth.

Calhoun, a South Carolinian and a states' rights man, at last responded to the President's toast: "The Union, next to our liberty, most dear. May we always remember that it can only be preserved by respecting the rights of the states and distributing equally the benefits and burdens of the Union." If the occasion provided little comfort to the states' righters, pro-Union forces across the nation, knowing that the President stood with them, took new heart.

(In delivering his famous toast, Jackson made a slip of the tongue. He intended to say, "Our Federal Union: It must be preserved," but he left out the word "Federal." Later he corrected himself to reporters, and the newspapers recorded for history what he had meant to say rather than what he had actually said.)

The battle over nullification did not end with a banquet and the drinking of toasts. South Carolina, vigorously opposed to a tariff law passed by Congress, set out to nullify it. In November of 1832 a special convention passed an ordinance which declared that the state would not be bound by the law. Federal officers were forbidden to collect any import duties in South Carolina after February 1, 1833. Moreover, declared the ordinance, if the Federal government tried to use force, South Carolina would secede from the Union.

President Jackson had begun making preparations as soon as there was a hint of trouble. The forts in Charleston harbor were alerted, warships were sent to the city and anchored with guns ready for action, and Major General Winfield Scott was put in command of army forces in the state. Then, on December 10, 1832, the President issued his Proclamation to the People of South Carolina, considered to be the greatest state paper of his eight years in office, indeed one of the greatest issued by any President. Jackson was firm without shaking his fist; he argued skillfully, appealing to the intelligence of the people of South Carolina, but he warned them that their course would lead to disaster.

Nullification, he said, was an "impractical absurdity." If it had been accepted when the nation was young, the Union would have broken up almost at once. No state could refuse to obey the law of the land, and no state could leave the Union—"Disunion by armed force is treason."

The nation supported Old Hickory with a tremendous burst of patriotism. There were speeches, parades, and bonfires. One state legislature after another declared itself opposed to nullification and secession. Even southern states condemned the action of South Carolina. But February 1, the day on which South Carolina in-

Even in his home state of South Carolina, Calhoun's stand on nullification drew opposition. Contesting the 1832 election was the pro-Jackson Union Party, whose candidates for Congress are listed on this poster.

STATE RIGHTS & UNION TICKET
CONGRESS
WASHINGTON
William Drayton

STATE SENATOR
James L. Petigru

REPRESENTATIVES

UNION

Judge D. E. Huger.   Rene Godard.

John J. Bulow.   Joel R. Poinsett.

John Strohecker.   C. G. Memminger.

Benj. F. Hunt.   Elias B. Hort.

John Johnson Jr.   H. A. Desaussure.

                           J. J. Pringle

H. S. Legare.   B. Y. Dunkin

William Aiken

UNION & LIBERTY ONE & INDIVISIBLE

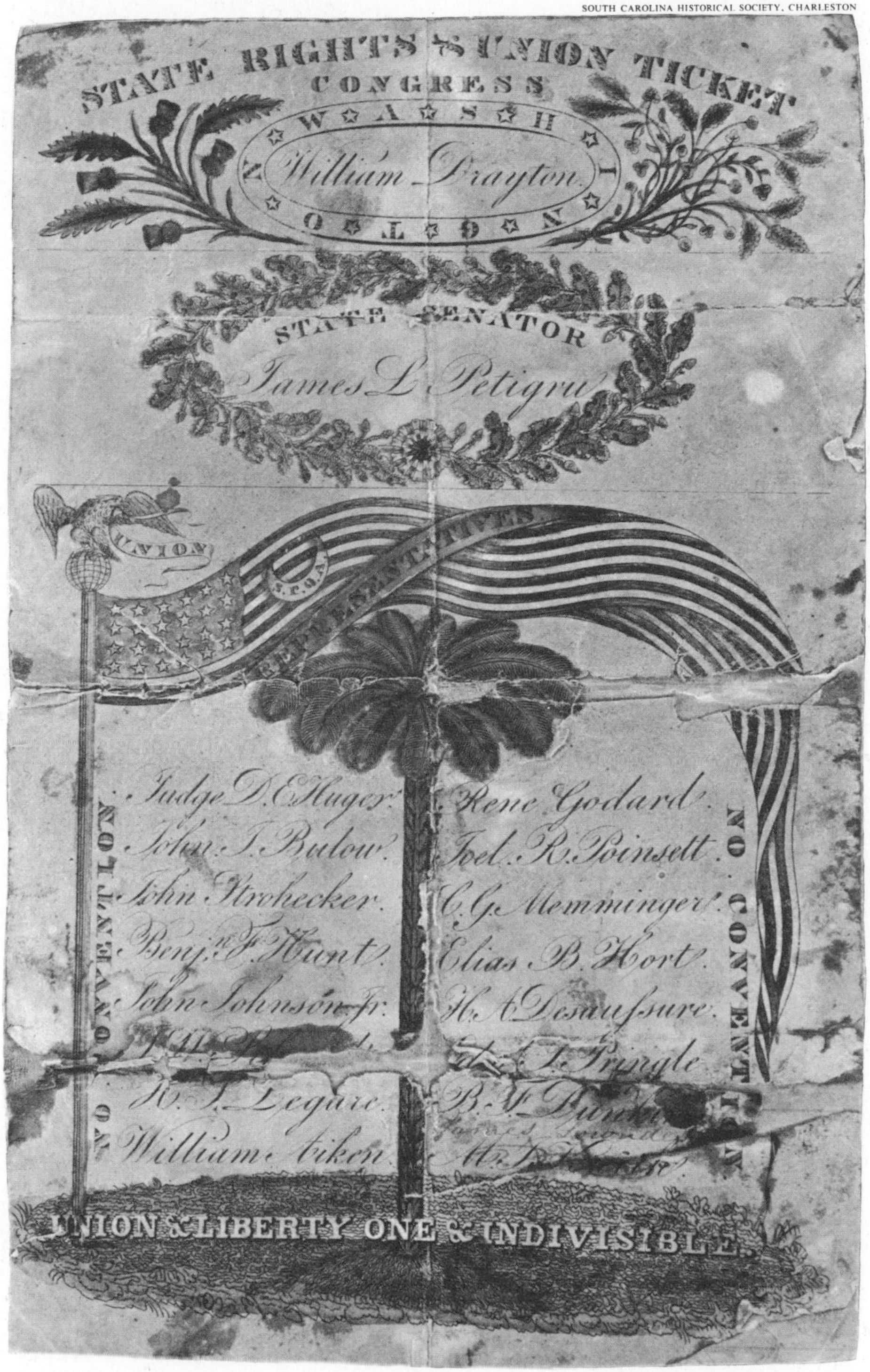

Cagey Martin Van Buren (left) helped Jackson phrase his statement opposing nullification, but then quietly backed out of the controversy to avoid inflaming his own political allies in the South. Van Buren was called "the Little Magician." Ex-President John Quincy Adams, old and tired when the daguerreotype above was taken in 1847, won a seat in Congress in 1832, just in time to attack Jackson for not dealing more harshly with the nullifiers.

"The bank," thundered Jackson, "is trying to kill me, but I will kill it!" Nicholas Biddle (left), the bank's president, bore the brunt of Old Hickory's assault by daring to make the issue a personal one. Although he was aided by the scowling presence of Daniel Webster (right), Biddle went down to defeat.

tended to halt the collection of all import duties within her borders, was fast approaching.

There was some serious doubt as to whether a President had the power to use the army and navy to enforce revenue laws; Jackson asked Congress for a "Force Bill" giving him the authority. But Congress argued and delayed, with John Calhoun, who had resigned as Vice President, leading the opposition. Jackson was ready to act anyway. He prepared to send troops into South Carolina and to call on the governors of the other states for more men.

On January 21, 1833, only ten days before the deadline, the nerves of the South Carolina nullifiers gave way, and they backed down. The nullification ordinance was suspended with the excuse that the state wanted to see what a new tariff bill, then being considered by Congress, would be like. On March 15, the nullification ordinance was withdrawn entirely.

Andrew Jackson had won another battle, and his popularity soared. Civil war had been prevented and the Union preserved—for a while, at least. The spirit of nullification and secession was not dead. Within thirty years that spirit would rise again throughout the entire South, helping to push

GENERAL JACKSON SLAYING THE MANY HEADED MONSTER.

The Second Bank is slain. With the stick of his veto and the assistance of Vice President Van Buren (center) and Major Jack Downing (right), a cartoon character of the day, Old Hickory dispatches all twenty-four branches of the "many headed monster." The largest is that of top-hatted Nicholas Biddle.

the nation into the tragedy of the Civil War.

Jackson did not always leap so quickly into the fight against nullification. The Cherokee Indians lived on lands within the state of Georgia which had been guaranteed to them by Federal treaty. They renounced warfare with the whites, and made great strides along the path toward civilization, inventing a system of writing their language, taking up farming, weaving, and other peaceful arts, and developing self-government for themselves. They were, if anything, better citizens than the Georgians eager to steal their land.

Georgia declared that its laws rather than Federal laws would henceforth govern the Cherokee lands. In 1832 the Indians went to the Supreme Court, which supported them; Georgia paid no attention to the court. The state had nullified Federal laws, but when the Cherokees asked Jackson to enforce the court's decision, he announced that he had no power to do so. Jackson seldom had trouble finding the power to do what he wanted, but he had no intention of defending Indians against white settlers. The Cherokees were pushed off the lands they had been promised forever, and forced to move across the Mississippi.

Andrew Jackson's administration, like every one before or since, had a great many problems to deal with, large and small, at home and in its dealings with other nations. But two issues rank high above all others in importance. One was the battle against nullification. The second was Jackson's fight against the Second Bank of the United States.

This institution, although privately owned and controlled, had been chartered in 1816 by the Federal government and was used by the Treasury for deposit of the government's money. By skillful management, the bank grew strong; it manipulated state banks in such a way as to make currency, that is, paper money, safer and more dependable than it had been before. With its many branches, it was even able to regulate the flow of business in an area by being generous or stingy with its loans and so keep a tight rein on the amount of money in circulation.

A great many people opposed the bank. They considered it a monopoly only in the interests of the wealthy and those who made it a business to loan money; they considered it undemocratic for a private institution to have so much power over the nation's economy. The government was urged to deposit its money in a number of state banks or in its own depository. There were also those, particularly among the workers in the East, who disliked any bank that had the power to issue paper money.

As a "hard-money" man, Andrew Jackson opposed the Second Bank and mistrusted its power. Although its charter did not expire until 1836, he let it be known as soon as he be-

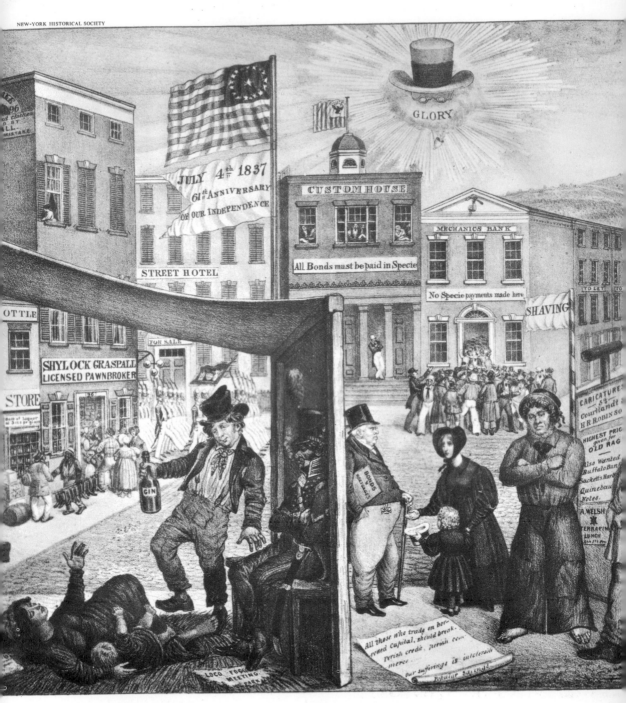

The shoeless workmen, idle businesses, and forlorn mothers in this piece of Whig propaganda on the Panic of 1837 represent the tragic results of the battle of the bank. Presiding over the scene of misery is the all-too-plain symbol of Andrew Jackson.

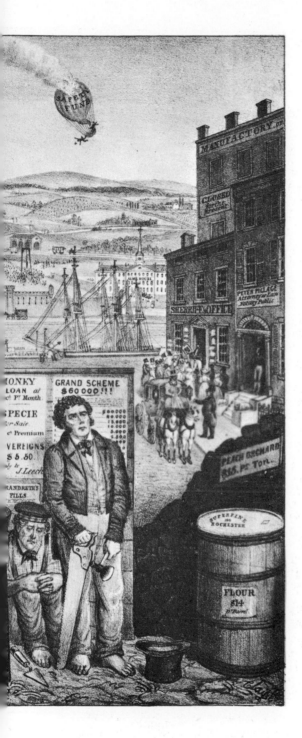

came President in 1829 that he was against renewing the charter.

Nicholas Biddle, the president of the bank, quickly made a political issue of the charter. Powerful men supported Biddle, men like Daniel Webster and Henry Clay. In the Presidential campaign of 1832, in which Clay ran against Jackson, the question of whether the Second Bank should be rechartered was a main campaign issue. Jackson won easily, with 219 electoral votes to 49 for Clay. Martin Van Buren, Jackson's short, shrewd former secretary of state, was elected Vice President.

His stand on the bank controversy won many votes for Old Hickory, and Jackson considered his overwhelming victory a sign that the people supported his attack on Mr. Biddle's bank. The President ordered his secretary of the treasury to begin removing government deposits from the bank and placing them in selected state banks—popularly called Jackson's "pet banks."

Nicholas Biddle fought back, using every trick he knew—and he knew a good many. The bank now handled its funds so that people found loans hard to get and money scarce; the resulting hard times were blamed on the President. But Jackson was too strong to be defeated. The Second Bank died as a national bank, as he had planned, when its charter expired in 1836. Although it was later chartered as a state bank in Pennsylvania, it went bankrupt within five years.

Jackson had fought the bank because it represented—to him—the aristocracy and the "money power" —a power out of place in his vision of a truly democratic republic. Many who supported him believed that small banks throughout the nation should have a chance to hold a share of the country's money.

On the other hand, Nicholas Biddle and his Second Bank had given the nation the strongest currency it had ever had—or would have again for a long time. The system of pet banks did not work well. With government money in their vaults, they felt safe in issuing large amounts of paper money. This money, in turn, was used to buy and sell land, the prices of which rose to ridiculous levels.

The bubble burst when President Jackson issued his Specie Circular in July, 1836, directing the government to accept only specie—gold or silver money—in payment for public lands. Since there was not enough of this "hard" money to replace more than a fraction of the paper money in circulation, land prices plummeted. This, in part, led to the Panic of 1837. Farm prices fell, unemployment rose, banks failed, and there were food riots among the poor in the cities. The effects of the panic did not disappear completely for five or six years.

Old Hickory, however, received none of the blame, for he was out of the White House and Martin Van Buren was President by the time the Panic of 1837 occurred.

Jackson had selected "Little Van," his former secretary of state and Vice President, as the man to follow him. By the election of 1836, the Jacksonian forces were everywhere known as Democrats. In contrast to 1824, when all four candidates were from the same party, the two-party system was now becoming firmly established. In opposition to the Jacksonians were the National Republicans, known after 1833 as the Whigs.

The Whigs could not agree on a candidate, so they put up three who were strong in different parts of the country, hoping that the election would be thrown into the House of Representatives. Daniel Webster was one, William Henry Harrison, an old Indian fighter (and later to be President) was another, and Hugh White from Jackson's own state of Tennessee was the third. But the Whig strategy failed, and Little Van was elected easily.

Jackson was ill, as he so often was now, during the last months of his Presidency. He ate his meals in bed and worked on a couch, trying to direct the packing and preparations for leaving. Gifts came in—a light carriage made of hickory, another made of wood from the great frigate *Constitution*, an enormous cartwheel of cheese four feet across and weighing 1,400 pounds, and any number of

A man who claimed he was the rightful heir to the British crown tried to assassinate the President in January of 1835. Both of the would-be killer's pistols misfired, and he was captured and declared insane.

pipes, hats, canes, and other odds and ends.

Andrew Jackson's last official act as President was to send to the Senate, on March 3, 1837, the nomination of a minister to the new Republic of Texas. The next day he drove in a coach to the Capitol with Van Buren for the inauguration. The crowds seemed more interested in the old man with the silvery hair, now only an ex-President, than they were in the new President of the United States.

Jackson spent the next day resting at the White House—a guest there now—and on March 6 he was driven in a coach to the railroad station to begin the long journey home to the Hermitage. Another of his many careers was at an end.

The Gentleman from Tennessee *was painted by Ralph
Earl, Jackson's constant companion at the Hermitage and
the White House. He called himself "the King's painter."*

The
Old Man of the Hermitage

7

Andrew Jackson was home again, this time to stay. But the people had not given him up. They had stood along the way to watch him pass on his homeward journey; now they sent letters to the Hermitage asking for a lock of his hair or a line of his handwriting, or just expressing their best wishes. Old Hickory was one of those rare Presidents who ended his term of office much more popular than when he began it; although he was hated by the wealthy classes he called the "neebobs," the common people's love for him grew steadily.

Andrew Jackson was more than just a popular and well-loved man now at the close of his career. In the judgment of history he was also a great President. His greatness was built on several things. A successful military career gave brightness to his name. Some of his acts as President greatly affected the course of

events—his handling of the nullification fight, for example, actually saved the Union.

Perhaps most important, Andrew Jackson revolutionized the Presidency. He was the first really strong President, increasing the strength and prestige of the office by exercising powers that Presidents before him had never dreamed of using. He was the leader of all the people, drawing his support not from any one region but from the nation as a whole. Instead of the many voices of Congress, the government of Jackson's time spoke with one voice—that of the President.

Jackson used all the power of the Presidency to attack head-on the great issues of the day—nullification, the Second Bank, the Indian problem. He exercised the veto power more frequently than all the previous Presidents put together, and he

Old Hickory's hand-picked successor, Martin Van Buren, handily won the election of 1836, only to inherit the shattering effects of the Panic of 1837. This post-election jibe at Jackson's Specie Circular bill, which doomed many banks, has Van Buren dutifully following his chief down the road of financial ruin.

made the role of party leader a vital part of the office. One other factor sets him apart from his predecessors —he helped bring about a basic change in the way American democracy works.

Jackson let the common people take part in government. Until his time, politicians were suspicious of the common man. Candidates were picked by political leaders in small, secret meetings called caucuses. A number of eastern states had property qualifications for voting to make sure that only solid citizens cast ballots.

In Jackson's day the country was changing fast; a new generation was not satisfied with the old undemocratic ways of doing things. Men were crossing the mountains and moving into the West, carving homes out of the wilderness with their own hands, getting along by what they did and not by who their fathers were. The constitutions of the new western states provided for what was, in those times, almost universal suffrage. Only women and Negroes were not allowed to vote.

It did not matter if a man spelled badly (as Jackson did) or could read or write at all, as long as he could fell a tree, shoot and skin a bear, make a stump speech, break a team of horses, or do something else useful.

These people felt themselves the equal of any merchant or banker or politician from the East, and they demanded that their voices be heard. Other men, workers in the new textile mills and factories that were springing up in the East and especially in New England, were also beginning to ask for a voice in their own government.

Andrew Jackson provided them with that voice. At last, they said, there was someone in the White House in whom they could put their faith. Jackson, in turn, had faith in the common man, considering him able to do anything to which he set his mind. He believed that the common man had the capabilities of holding any office. Feeling as he did, he brought him into participation in the government for the first time, completing what Thomas Jefferson had started to do and making the American system at last truly democratic. His concept of rule by the common man is still known as Jacksonian Democracy, and the period of history when his ideas prevailed is known as the Jacksonian Era.

But Andrew Jackson, getting acquainted again with his fields and orchards at the Hermitage, was probably spending little time thinking about his place in history. He was seventy when he returned to Tennessee, and very weary, yet his plans to spend his remaining years in peace quickly turned into a cruel mockery.

Andrew, Jr. had taken over the management of the Hermitage during the last years of his father's Presidency, but he had not done well with the job. When he bought land he paid twice what it was worth. The cotton crops failed to turn out as large as young

Andrew had predicted. The price per pound was less than it should have been because the quality was poor.

Now, back home and trying to put everything in order, Jackson soon found that his son had mishandled other things as well. Hoping to begin the year 1838 free from debt, Jackson had to spend about $7,000 to meet all his bills. Most of that sum went to pay off the notes of other men which Andrew, Jr. had endorsed —that is, promised to repay if the person who had borrowed the money fell on hard times. Now the men whose debts he had guaranteed had not paid, and Old Hickory was left to make good the notes.

Nevertheless, the situation at the Hermitage looked promising, with prospects for a profit. Jackson bought a property called Halcyon Plantation on the Mississippi River and turned it over to his son to manage. He was sure young Andrew had learned from his mistakes and would do a good job.

Soon other liabilities began to turn up unexpectedly. There was the matter of $550 for a carriage bought by Andrew, Jr. two years before and never paid for. Then the financial collapse of one of Tennessee's richest men, a close friend of the Jacksons, revealed that young Andrew had endorsed a number of the man's notes and had also piled up other debts his father knew nothing about. Old Hickory gathered what funds he could in a hurry—selling some of his land, drawing an advance on his coming cotton crop, or by borrowing—and met the most pressing of the debts.

He tried to learn from his son how much he owed in all; the young man thought rather vaguely that it would be about $6,000. It soon turned out to be $12,000. Jackson was able to raise enough additional money to pay it all off.

Yet in spite of all the cause he had been given to lose his temper and shake his son until his teeth rattled, Andrew Jackson apparently never said a harsh word to him. He loved the young man and forgave him his troubles and failures, blaming most of them on the scheming men who took advantage of him.

Constantly pressed as he was with debts that seemed endless, and growing a little weaker and more bedeviled by sickness each year, the old man nevertheless remained in close touch with political affairs. In 1840 the Whigs ran William Henry Harrison, an old Indian fighter and general in the War of 1812, against Van Buren. Jackson stumped Tennessee for Little Van, something he had never done on his own behalf. It was not enough; Van Buren lost the election, failing even to carry Tennessee. Harrison died after a month in office, and was succeeded by Vice President John Tyler.

Meanwhile, Jackson had not seen the last of his son's debts. He had to sell three of his race horses, along with other things, to raise money, but the demands for payment kept com-

Andrew Jackson, Jr., painted at about twenty-two by Earl, cast a dark shadow over his father's retirement by running up a huge backlog of debts.

The gaily-colored handkerchief above was displayed by William Henry Harrison's supporters in the 1840 election. Harrison neither lived in a log cabin nor was born in one, but Whigs used the symbol anyway.

James Polk's narrow victory over Clay in 1844 prompted the cartoon at right, in which a relieved Jackson announces from the clouds, "My country is saved!" Below him is a somber Whig funeral procession.

ing in. By the beginning of 1841 they amounted to $3,000 over and above the $12,000 Old Hickory had paid not long before. Then it became evident that young Andrew was getting along badly at Halcyon Plantation in Mississippi; there was not enough food for the slaves, and the manager was suing for back wages.

In this dark time, three of Jackson's friends offered loans on the easiest terms the proud old man would accept, and once more he paid off all his obligations. Young Andrew had

been "swindled and imposed upon," he said (as he had said so many times), but he was sure (as he had been before) that now his son had learned his lesson.

"I have been brought low with a severe attack of chills and fevers," Jackson wrote to a friend in 1842. He was reporting such illnesses more and more often, and his eyesight was failing. But these ailments did not slow down his political activities. He wrote letters constantly, offering advice, making suggestions, asking questions.

When the issue of annexing the Republic of Texas became an urgent matter in Washington, he became fearful that it might not be approved. At the beginning of the campaign of 1844, his long-time political associate, Martin Van Buren, announced that he was opposed to annexation; as a result, Jackson welcomed the nomination of James Polk as the Democratic candidate.

Old Hickory never found the tranquility he longed for, yet with all its cares and worries, life at the

Hermitage had many pleasant hours. He was a farmer at heart and enjoyed the cycle of planting, growth, and harvest. Good friends frequently stopped by for long discussions of politics and the latest happenings in Tennessee and Washington. There were always nephews and nieces—and now grandnephews and grandnieces —to enliven the big house. And one of his greatest comforts was his daily visit to Rachel's grave in the Hermitage garden.

But in the end he always had to fight his debts. The Mississippi flooded, washing out the cotton crop at Halcyon Plantation and drowning many of the animals. Incredibly, young Andrew had somehow managed to run up new debts of $6,000. Staunch friends heard of Old Hickory's latest troubles and wrote to him that, since they owed all their own success to him, he could draw on them for any amount up to $100,000. Once again he was able to pay off the creditors.

It was past the middle of March, 1845, when Old Hickory paid off the latest pile of debts; only a few weeks were left to him, for even his iron will could not prevail forever against a body worn out. One lung was wasted away from tuberculosis and the other

Failing rapidly, his features contorted into a prolonged grimace, Old Hickory allowed himself to be photographed at the Hermitage in 1845. Soon afterward, the long life of the soldier-statesman was finished.

was badly infected. He was blind in one eye, and his body was beginning to swell with dropsy.

In June, as spring drifted into summer along the Cumberland, it was plain that Andrew Jackson had seen his last turning of the seasons. He was unable to move from his chair to his bed without being lifted, and he was in pain most of the time, but he still had things to do. When he asked Andrew, Jr. how things were going on the two plantations, his son told the dying old man that some money was badly needed. Jackson, as one of his last acts, wrote a letter asking for a loan of another $2,000 for his son.

The next day he wrote a letter to President Polk, advising him to veto a plan to pay off at face value certain paper money, the actual value of which had fallen badly. It was not the kind of letter that comes from an enfeebled and wandering mind, although the physical strain of writing it exhausted him. It was his last letter. Two days later, Sunday, June 8, 1845, the end came for Andrew Jackson.

Death came slowly and with dignity. He said good-by to all the servants, and gave his blessing to each member of his family. An old friend or two came into his room and exchanged farewells, but only briefly, for Old Hickory was very, very tired.

At six o'clock, long before the late-setting June sun had sunk behind the western hills, he died quietly. The warrior had laid down his sword, the statesman had put aside his pen.

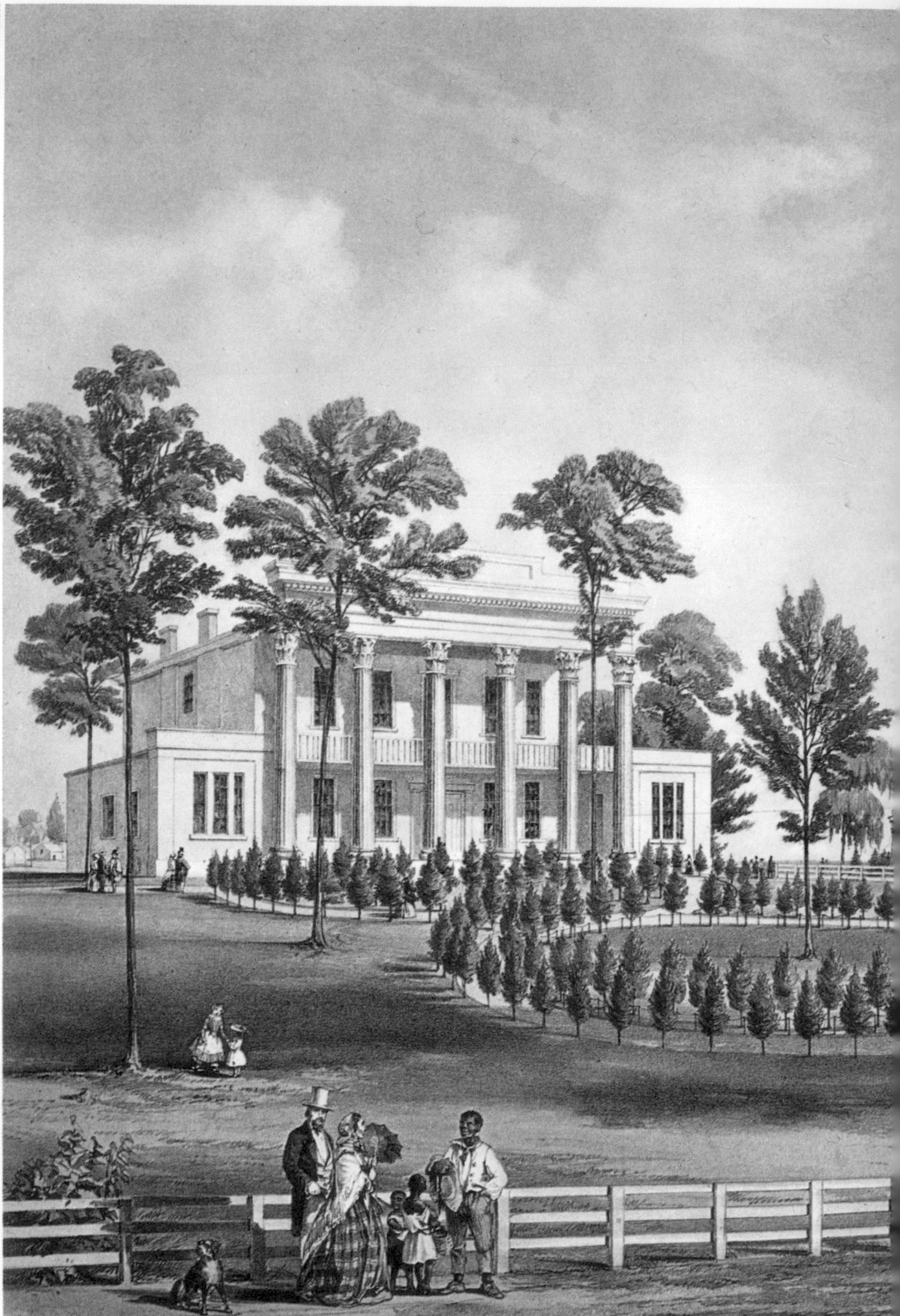

Jackson's Hermitage remains today unchanged from the classic structure depicted in this 1856 print. It ranks with Washington's Mount Vernon, which inspired its design, and Jefferson's Monticello as the finest of the early Presidents' homes.

Canvassing for votes.

AMERICAN HERITAGE PUBLISHING CO., INC.

PRESIDENT JAMES PARTON

EDITORIAL DIRECTOR JOSEPH J. THORNDIKE, JR.

EDITOR, BOOK DIVISION RICHARD M. KETCHUM

ART DIRECTOR IRWIN GLUSKER

AMERICAN HERITAGE JUNIOR LIBRARY

EDITOR STEPHEN W. SEARS

ART DIRECTOR EMMA LANDAU

ASSISTANT EDITOR DENNIS A. DINAN

CHIEF PICTURE RESEARCHER JULIA B. POTTS

PICTURE RESEARCHER MARY LEVERTY

EDITORIAL ASSISTANT AMY L. RHODES

COPY EDITOR PATRICIA COOPER

ACKNOWLEDGMENTS

The Editors wish to thank the following individuals and organizations for their assistance and for making available pictorial material in their collections:

Mrs. Anne S. K. Brown, Providence
Chicago Historical Society—Mrs. Mary Frances Rhymer
Corcoran Gallery of Art, Washington—Mrs. Mary H. Forbes
Fogg Art Museum, Harvard University—Agnes Mongan
Colonel Edgar William and Bernice Chrysler Garbisch, New York
Stanley F. Horn, Nashville
Ladies' Hermitage Association, Nashville—Martha Lindsay
Lawson McGhee Library, Knoxville—Pollyanna Creekmore
Library of Congress, Washington—Virginia Daiker
Museum of Fine Arts, Boston—Elizabeth P. Riegel
National Gallery of Art, Washington—Huntington Cairns
New-York Historical Society—Betty Jane Ezequelle
New York Public Library—Mrs. Maud Cole, Paul Rugen
Franklin D. Roosevelt Library, Hyde Park, N.Y.
Tennessee Historical Society, Nashville—Robert T. Quarles, Jr.

The photographs on pages 127 and 133, from the Metropolitan Museum of Art, are the gifts of I. N. Phelps Stokes, Edward S. Hawes, Alice Mary Hawes, and Marion Augusta Hawes (1937). The drawing on page 14, also from the Metropolitan, is the gift of Robert de Forest (1906). The prints on pages 15 and 53 are reproduced through the courtesy of Harry Shaw Newman.

FOR FURTHER READING

Bass, Robert D. *Swamp Fox*. Henry Holt & Co., 1959.

Brooks, Charles B. *The Siege of New Orleans*. University of Washington Press, 1961.

Chambers, William Nisbet. *Old Bullion Benton*. Little, Brown, 1956.

Coit, Margaret L. *John C. Calhoun, American Patriot*. Houghton Mifflin, 1950.

Daniels, Jonathan. *The Devil's Backbone, The Story of the Natchez Trace*. McGraw-Hill, 1962.

Goggin, John M. *Osceola*. University of Florida Press, 1958.

Govan, Thomas. *Nicholas Biddle*. University of Chicago Press, 1959.

Horn, Stanley F. *The Hermitage*. Greenberg, 1950.

James, Marquis. *Andrew Jackson: The Border Captain*. Bobbs-Merrill, 1933.

James, Marquis. *Andrew Jackson: Portrait of a President*. Bobbs-Merrill, 1937.

Jensen, Amy La Follette. *The White House and Its Thirty-two Families*. McGraw-Hill, 1958.

Parton, James. *Life of Andrew Jackson*. Houghton Mifflin, 1888.

Schlesinger, Arthur M., Jr. *The Age of Jackson*. Little, Brown, 1950.

Stone, Irving. *President's Lady*. Doubleday, 1959.

Thayer, Theodore. *Nathanael Greene*. Twayne Publishers, 1960.

Tucker, Glenn. *Poltroons and Patriots*. Bobbs-Merrill, 1954.

Tunis, Edwin. *Frontier Living*. World Publishing Co., 1961.

Van Deusen, Glyndon G. *The Jacksonian Era*. Harper & Brothers, 1959.

White, Leonard D. *The Jacksonians*. Macmillan, 1954.

Woodward, Grace Steele. *The Cherokees*. University of Oklahoma Press, 1963.

Index

Bold face indicates pages on which illustrations appear